"Barry Hudock's account of the life and work of John Courtney Murray shows that the development of Catholic teaching on religious liberty cannot be reduced to abstract, numbered paragraphs in an encyclical or catechism. It is a riveting story of clashing personalities, impossible possibilities, and hope against all hope. It is the story of the Holy Spirit at work in the church."

—M. Cathleen Kaveny
Darald and Juliet Libby Professor
Boston College

Struggle, Condemnation, Vindication

*John Courtney Murray's
Journey toward Vatican II*

Barry Hudock

Foreword by
Drew Christiansen, SJ

A Michael Glazier Book

LITURGICAL PRESS
Collegeville, Minnesota

www.litpress.org

A Michael Glazier Book published by Liturgical Press

Cover design by Monica Bokinskie.
Portrait of John Courtney Murray by Jamel Akib.

Excerpts from documents of the Second Vatican Council are from *Vatican Council II: The Conciliar and Postconciliar Documents*, edited by Austin Flannery, OP, © 1996. Used with permission of Liturgical Press, Collegeville, Minnesota.

Excerpts from "Leo XIII: Separation of Church and State" by John Courtney Murray in *Theological Studies* 14 (June 1953): 145–214. Used by permission of SAGE Publications.

1   2   3   4   5   6   7   8   9

Library of Congress Cataloging-in-Publication Data

Hudock, Barry.
    Struggle, condemnation, vindication : John Courtney Murray's journey
toward Vatican II / Barry Hudock.
        pages   cm
        "A Michael Glazier Book."
        Includes bibliographical references.
        ISBN 978-0-8146-8322-4 — ISBN 978-0-8146-8347-7 (ebook)
        1. Murray, John Courtney.   2. Catholics—Biography.
    3. Theologians—United States—Biography.   I. Title.
    BX4705.M977H83   2015
    230'.2092—dc23
    [B]   2014035587

This is dedicated to Barb Aimino, Geoff Brown, Cheri Graham, Laura Guidice, Tina Havrilla, Shawn Iadonato, Alicia Kopas, Doug LaMarca, Penny Learn, Arley Lewis, Dave Lishinsky, Sheila Pearce, Ed Skarbek, and Birgit Voll. I miss you guys.

And also to my wife Antoinette and our lively crew: Abigail, Cecilia, Nicholas, Hope, Gianna, Jacob, and Brittany. Vi amo, tutti.

Contents

Part Four: Vindication and Vatican II

Foreword

"Civilization is formed by men [*sic*] locked together in argument." The line belongs to the late Dominican scholar Thomas Gilbey. It dramatizes a lesson Gilbey, a twentieth-century historian of medieval social and political thought, learned from medieval Scholasticism. Namely, ideas grow and develop, are qualified, controverted, refined, distorted—and sometimes reemerge—in a continuous argument across the generations. That kind of argument, Gilbey believed, was Scholasticism at its best. An idea does not become real until it has been refined in argument with others.

A Life in Dialogue

John Courtney Murray cited Gilbey's line about "men locked together in argument" in the opening essay of his 1960 book *We Hold These Truths*, "The Civilization of the Pluralist Society." In that book, Murray's interlocutors were proponents, like himself, of the Catholic natural law tradition in dialogue with its critics: contemporary Protestants like Reinhold Niebuhr, Robert McAfee Brown, and Julian Hartt; classic Anglo-American political thinkers like John Locke and the American Founding Fathers; legal theorists like Adolf Berle; and militant secularists like Sidney Hook.

Secular liberals were the targets of Murray's sharpest criticism. "Barbarians," he called them, for "corrupting the inherited wisdom by which the people have always lived and creating a climate of doubt and bewilderment in which clarity about the larger aims of life are dimmed." Murray's controversialist style, evident in this quotation from *We Hold These Truths*, was colored, no doubt, by the study of scholastic philosophy with its responses to *adversarii* who held alternative or erroneous positions. In Murray's time at Woodstock College, the Jesuit major seminary where he taught, students were still invited to do public defenses of disputed questions (*quaestiones disputatae*) in which fending off opposing positions was essential to the performance.

One irony of the history of ideas is that, among today's Catholic sectarians and proponents of Radical Orthodoxy, Murray's political theology is mischaracterized as a Catholic sellout to liberal American culture. In Murray's own day, however, he defended the Catholic tradition against secular liberalism, what we today call "libertarianism." At the same time, he endeavored to persuade his fellow Catholics and Americans at large of the congruence between the idea of limited government in medieval Catholic political thought and the American constitutional principle of separation of church and state.

Contrary to his critics, on many issues Murray was a political and social conservative, esteeming "the ordered freedom" advocated by traditionalist conservatives like Russell Kirk. He often sounded like Edmund Burke. Public consensus is sustained, he believed, by a balance of reason and custom. When people "live together according to reason," he wrote, "reason is embodied in law and custom, and incorporated in a web of institutions that sufficiently reveal rational influences, though they are not, and cannot be wholly rational."

Present-day readers should bear in mind that Murray was a twentieth-century natural law thinker, educated before the biblical revival and the ecumenism that followed Vatican II. Those currents of thought informed the thinking of some of his European collaborators at Vatican II, like the French Dominican Yves Congar. Whereas Murray's natural law political theology defines the first chapter of the Declaration on Religious Liberty, Congar's more pastoral and biblically informed theological style can be seen in the formulas of the second chapter. The parallel expositions within the one document are an accurate reflection of a critical stage in the evolution of the church's political-moral thought at the time of the council. While Murray worked amicably with the proponents of this new style of theology, he nonetheless stood staunchly by his own approach, and his later writing shows no evidence of being influenced by the newer European schools of thought.

By my own lights, Murray's theological method was imperfect. I too would have preferred that he had given more attention to biblical theology. In hindsight, it is not clear that neutral-sounding natural law language has been any more persuasive to those outside the Catholic community, as Murray believed, than the biblical-pastoral language of the French school. Some of the American critics of Catholic intolerance then and now, it should be recalled, are fundamentalist Protestants for whom Scripture is common ground. In the fifty years that have passed since the promulgation of *Dignitatis Humanae*, moreover, under Evangelical influence, Scripture has often served in the United States as the intellectual background for public debate on religion.

All the same, for mid-century American Catholics Murray's natural law political theology facilitated their inclusion in the American mainstream; and for the universal church it opened the way to new esteem for freedom of religion and liberty of individual conscience everywhere. Indeed, in Murray's later advocacy of selective conscientious objection (SCO) to military service, he labored ahead of his time for an application of the principle of liberty of conscience in relation to political obligation. Murray's present-day Catholic pacifist critics have made SCO a field for active programming among today's volunteer military personnel. While those pacifist critics support SCO out of their commitment to nonviolence, Murray defended it as a necessary corollary of the Catholic Just War Tradition.

Murray was a Catholic churchman in the Jesuit tradition. He believed that the Catholic Church had a role to play in public life. While in the seventeenth century that meant Jesuits served as confessors to kings, in the modern, American context it meant contributing to national debate. Murray helped build the intellectual platform from which the US bishops in the 1980s would teach their fellow Americans to think ethically about war, nuclear deterrence, and economic justice. For Murray, taking responsibility for the world and exercising an inclusive care for Christians of very different degrees and forms of religious commitment—the distinguishing marks of Ernst Troeltsch's "church" type religious community—were commitments central to Catholic identity. The purist aspirations of his critics are more aligned with marks of the opposing "sect" type, fidelity to a perfectionist ethic in a narrow community of the elect.

A Rolling Argument

I first learned of John Murray with the publication of the *Time* magazine cover story "U.S. Catholics and the State" in December 1960. Boris Chaliapin's portrait, which hangs today in the foyer of America Press in New York, showed an austere, almost-Olympian Murray gazing out from the cover. He appeared the very image of intellectual authority. An impressionable fifteen-year-old, I immediately added *We Hold These Truths* to my Christmas wish-list. I read it then and reread it. I read it in college, once more in theology, and again as a young seminary professor. As much as Murray's defense of the American Proposition of limited government, the quote from Gilbey stood out in my adolescent imagination. In Murray's engagement with his American adversaries, the life of the mind as what the Greeks called *logomachy*, a war of arguments, took on life for me. The Gilbey-Murray vision of civilization as a rolling argument has remained with me ever since.

In the United States Murray became a celebrity intellectual. He lectured at Yale, partied with Henry and Claire Booth Luce, and advised presidential candidate Jack Kennedy, but in the Catholic world Murray was engaged in a high-stakes, rough-and-tumble argument with unforgiving opponents. This argument took place in theological journals and in backchannel communications with Vatican officials. Even as Murray was feted by *Time* for reconciling Catholic faith with American freedom, he labored under a yoke of silence in deference to his Jesuit superiors in Rome. He was firmly discouraged from publishing on religious freedom, the topic to which his research and writing had been dedicated. For the better part of a decade, he withdrew from the contest of ideas.

In *Struggle, Condemnation, Vindication* Barry Hudock has written a surefooted account of the extended argument over religious liberty in which Murray engaged for more than twenty years. Murray's struggle led eventually to the Second Vatican Council's Declaration on Religious Liberty and the vindication of Murray's thesis that the religious liberty provided by the American Bill of Rights has its roots in the Catholic natural law tradition. Hudock shows how the Catholic conversation over religious freedom was a conversation across the centuries with Gelasius, Aquinas, Bellarmine, and Leo XIII, as well as a conversation between Murray and his contemporaries, Francis Connell, Joseph

Francis Fenton, and Cardinal Alfredo Ottaviani. Hudock ably chronicles Murray's intellectual evolution from a defender of the traditional Roman position that favored church establishment as the ideal, through his historical investigations of various historical constructions of the church-state question, to his forthright advocacy of religious liberty as integral to the natural law tradition.

A Contest of Ideas

Barry Hudock's treatment of Murray's intellectual career is itself a narrative of a contest of ideas. While Murray is the focus and his vindication at the Second Vatican Council comes as the culmination of the work, Hudock treats Murray's opponents, especially Connell and Fenton, with evenhanded respect. The book records the unfolding of their decades-long argument over religious liberty with reportorial clarity and scholarly sensitivity. He also faithfully records their disillusionment not just with the council's decisions on religious liberty but also with the whole reforming project of Vatican II. For me, a special virtue of the book is its exposition of the Roman debate over the topic, which had been for me, not a specialist in the field, still a hazy matter.

The adversaries' dispute with Murray was, in addition to being an argument over religious liberty, a hermeneutical contest over the respective roles of theological argument and magisterial authority in church teaching. Was the received doctrine on church and state immutable truth, or was it a conversation over mutable formulations of an eternal truth? Does history matter in the formulation of doctrine? Should the mere repetition of an earlier position be regarded as authoritative? How should theological arguments be received when they seem to diverge from authoritative magisterial judgments? When is the dictum *Roma locuta est, causa finita est* ("Rome has spoken, the case is closed") no longer applicable? These larger, hermeneutical questions still demand scholarly reflection and intra-ecclesial dialogue.

In recent years, Murray's advocacy of religious liberty has taken on new life with the worldwide struggle for religious freedom. While that debate is sometimes colored by the antipathies of the American culture wars, Murray's life work was decisive in placing Catholicism firmly on the side of freedom. Two decades ago when I worked at the US bishops' conference, the office inquired of the Vatican about running a campaign on behalf of imprisoned priests abroad. The response was telling, "Yes, but be sure to advocate on behalf of all believers." Murray, who, Hudock tells us, in his last years grew tired of theological discussion of religious freedom, would still have been proud. Even at the seat of Roman authority the ideal of religious liberty had been thoroughly appropriated.

Hudock's Lesson

There are many lessons to be drawn from John Courtney Murray's struggle for the Catholic Church's acceptance of religious liberty. I have focused on one, the ongoing nature of theological argument. Barry Hudock draws a somewhat different and wise lesson:

> One thing the story of John Courtney Murray and his struggle for the truth of religious freedom teaches us is that understanding the truth about God and God's revelation to humanity is sometimes a struggle. That revelation and what it means in the circumstances of our day (and any day) is not always clear and not easily discernible—even by those whose job it is to discern it.

Accordingly, Hudock concludes with a plea for cognitive humility by theologians and prelates. "It seems we need to be a little more patient with one another," he writes, "and more cautious in our judgments about our own thinking and that of others." In a time when the pope asks, "Who am I to judge?" Catholic intellectuals, bishops, and theologians should find it less difficult to hold their theological animus in check.

The Ongoing Argument

The conversation on religious freedom continues. Today's debates take place primarily in two fields: domestic health policy and international human rights policy. There is yet a third issue that still requires theological investigation, namely, freedom in the church.

In the United States the tensions between the US Conference of Catholic Bishops, some Catholic institutions, and other religious groups, especially Evangelicals, with the Obama administration over healthcare reform have narrowed to rather special claims, particularly whether the requirement to apply for an exemption to the healthcare mandate imposes a burden on religious liberty. That debate has strained what is left of traditional moral theology. It appears to have made inoperative the revered distinction of "remote material cooperation." In the name of freedom to uphold the church's teaching, moreover, a handful of bishops have even questioned the principle of the primacy of conscience in the moral life. Constitutionally, in adjudicating the dispute over "the mandate" to purchase health insurance, the US Supreme Court has extended the umbrella of religious freedom to cover privately owned businesses, an unexpected jurisprudential development.

The settled outcomes of these new questions are not yet clear. Pope Francis, for his part, has voiced reservations that a narrow set of moral concerns have seemed to supersede the proclamation of the Gospel. The US bishops and elements of the religious liberty lobby, however, continue to press those issues. The argument goes on.

On the international scene, there has seldom been a time since the Holocaust when religious minorities have been so much under attack in so many places. Christians have been driven from a large part of the Middle East. Sunnis are under threat in Iraq, and Shiites are persecuted in Pakistan and Afghanistan and elsewhere, including the so-called Islamic State. Muslim-Christian hostilities have grown across Africa as well. In Nigeria and Cameroon, Boko-Haram has been the antagonist, but in the Central African Republic Christian militias have been significant offenders. In China, where there have been long-standing difficulties, Rome and Beijing are feeling their way toward a possible rapprochement, perhaps beginning with renewed cooperation in the appointment of bishops. In the United States progress has been made toward institutionalizing religious liberty in both domestic and diplomatic policymaking. Religious freedom has been on the agendas of international agencies as well. But the gulf between aspiration and effective protection of religious minorities is still great.

Finally, there remains the application of the principles of religious liberty to the church itself. A clarification of hierarchal pastoral authority still needs to be developed in light of human dignity, the right to religious liberty, and the rights of the baptized in the church, all principles advanced by Vatican II that still need to be fully applied in canon law and pastoral practice.

The Church in the Culture of Encounter

Thanks to Vatican II's promulgation of *Dignitatis Humanae* Murray's legacy will be a lasting one in what mattered most to him, the principle of religious freedom. What remains in dispute today with Murray's contemporary critics is the stance the church takes toward the world. Do the times demand she take on a consistently countercultural, prophetic role? Or can she continue to make common cause with those whom the magisterial tradition calls "men and women of goodwill"?

In *Lumen Gentium* and *Gaudium et Spes* the council envisaged an interpenetration of church and world in a "Christ-transforming-culture" ecclesiology. Today Pope Francis has provided us with a unique model of church that is at once evangelical (missionary) and dialogical, committed to encounter with the world. In his apostolic exhortation The Joy of the Gospel, Pope Francis professes that acting through the world the Spirit teaches the church and that in dialogue with a range of cultures Christians can create "new syntheses" of Christian culture.

Contemporary critiques of Murray are rooted in a belief that in engaging with the world the church is inevitably compromised, whereas when it is true to itself and adheres to a distinctively Christian ethic, it will withhold itself in moral purity from the world or culture, the opposite of Pope Francis's church of the streets "where accidents happen." Francis demonstrates that the church can uphold a demanding Christian ethic while engaging with and learning from the world. Pope Francis's church-of-encounter model transcends the church-sect divide.

Thus, on the issues of church and world as on the question of religious freedom, the argument moves on. Not just civilization but the well-being of the church depends on it. Murray and Gilbey, both students of the history of theology, would surely understand.

Drew Christiansen, SJ
Georgetown University
January 15, 2015

Acknowledgments

I want to express my thanks to:

- Lisette Matano and the staff at Georgetown University Library's Special Collections Research Center
- Jane Stoeffler, Mike Dobbs, and the staff at The Catholic University of America's American Catholic Research Center and Archives
- Kate Feighery and Fr. Michael Morris of the archives of the Archdiocese of New York
- Jamel Akib, creator of the fine Murray portrait on the cover
- Drew Christiansen, SJ, who wrote the insightful introduction
- the many fine folks at Liturgical Press—too many to name—whose skills and professionalism have helped to make this book an exciting reality

Acknowledgments

Introduction

There have certainly been American Catholics more famous than John Courtney Murray; Dorothy Day and Archbishop Fulton Sheen come to mind. There have been more powerful ones, too, on both the ecclesial and secular landscapes; Cardinal Francis Spellman and President John F. Kennedy are good examples. But consider this: *No American Catholic has—by a long shot—had greater impact on the doctrinal beliefs of the global Roman Catholic Church than Fr. John Courtney Murray, SJ.*

With almost no power to wield and not much more fame (though he did once make the cover of *Time* magazine), John Courtney Murray influenced in a dramatic and (on these shores) unparalleled way the content of the doctrine that the church proposes to the faithful throughout the world to be believed and lived out daily.

When Murray stepped onto the ecclesial scene, the Catholic Church had a very clear teaching on the topic of religious freedom. To suggest that all human beings had such a right was deemed, well, "absurd." [1] After Murray, and thanks in part (though admittedly not solely) to him, the same church officially embraced religious freedom, and pope after pope has vigorously promoted it as—in the words of Pope Francis—"a fundamental human right" and "a path to peace in our troubled world." [2]

---

[1] Gregory XVI, encyclical letter *Mirari Vos* (1832), Papal Encyclicals Online, http://www.papalencyclicals.net/Greg16/g16mirar.htm.

[2] Francis, encyclical letter *Evangelii Gaudium* (2013), 255, 257, http://w2.vatican .va/content/francesco/en/apost_exhortations/documents/papa-francesco_esortazione -ap_20131124_evangelii-gaudium.html. Besides *Dignitatis Humanae*, the Second Vatican Council's Declaration on Religious Freedom, which we will consider at length below, see also, for example, John Paul II's encyclical letter *Redemptor Hominis* (1979), 17, http://www.vatican.va/holy_father/john_paul_ii/encyclicals/documents/hf_jp-ii _enc_04031979_redemptor-hominis_en.html, and Benedict XVI's *Message for the World Day of Peace 2011*, http://www.vatican.va/holy_father/benedict_xvi/messages /peace/documents/hf_ben-xvi_mes_20101208_xliv-world-day-peace_en.html.

While some American Catholics of a certain age—those in or nearing their golden years at this writing—may recognize Murray's name, most younger ones, unfortunately, know little of him. Coming into this research, I was among the latter, despite several years of advanced theological studies in early adulthood at some of the finest Catholic institutions.

But we *should* know him. For several important reasons, we ought not forget. Here are six:

1. "John Courtney Murray is the most significant Catholic theologian the church in the United States has ever produced."[3] Some voices worthy of a hearing have gone even further, to say he was "the finest"[4] and "the most outstanding"[5] we have had, and there is good reason for those statements, though others might demur. But there is no room for argument that he was and remains the most significant.

2. Though not single-handedly, Murray prompted, through his theological work, a historic rethinking of Catholic doctrine, expressed most notably in an important conciliar document. Indeed, the council itself explicitly recognized its teaching on religious freedom as a development of the teaching of previous popes (see *Dignitatis Humanae*, 1), and it was a *development* that looked to many, before its official approval, very much like a *contradiction* of past teaching. As this book will demonstrate, it did not come easily. "No other Vatican II document was as controversial and also none (even the document on the Jews to which *Dignitatis Humanae* was often linked) underwent so many revisions and machinations to keep it from coming to a vote. No other document involved so many direct and indirect papal interventions by Paul VI."[6]

[3] Robert W. McElroy, "He Held These Truths," *America* 192 (February 7, 2005), available at http://www.americamagazine.org/content/article.cfm?article_id=3995.

[4] Joseph A. Komonchak, "John Courtney Murray," in *The Encyclopedia of American Catholic History*, ed. Michael Glazier and Thomas J. Shelley (Collegeville, MN: Liturgical Press, 1997), 993–96, at 996.

[5] Charles Curran, *American Catholic Social Ethics: Twentieth-Century Approaches* (Notre Dame, IN: University of Notre Dame Press, 1982), 232.

[6] John Coleman "The Achievement of Religious Freedom," *U.S. Catholic Historian* 24, no. 1 (Winter 2006): 21–32, at 26.

3. Though the United States had not yet celebrated its bicentennial at the time, Murray brought about, despite powerful opposition, the first significant contribution of the unique experience of its people to the doctrinal life of the Catholic Church. *Dignitatis Humanae*, the council's Declaration on Religious Freedom, of which Murray was a central architect, clearly represents what may be called—as one bishop who was there put it—the "American contribution to the council."[7]

4. The theological-doctrinal drama in which Murray was engaged teaches us the important lesson that the meaning of God's revelation is not always clear, even to those with the charism of interpreting and teaching it. How that revelation applies to particular situations and circumstances throughout the various ages and eras of human history is sometimes even more difficult to say.

5. Religious liberty is currently a controversial and unquestionably important topic in the United States. The role of religion in a democracy and the best and most just relationship between church and state are questions that touch the moral foundations of our society. Murray helps us understand the nature and boundaries of that role.

6. To our deeply divided church, Murray's story offers a unifying bridge.

I pause to offer a few words of elaboration on this final point, because the polarization of the church, especially in the United States, is so troubling and because Murray so clearly transcends it.

Murray's story is one that "conservatives" (or traditionalists, or whatever the label) can cheer for. He was self-consciously faithful to Catholic tradition, willing to affirm without hesitation that the Catholic Church is the one true church founded by Christ. Though critics claimed his work ran contrary to the magisterium, Murray never suggested that this was an unimportant criticism. Indeed, it was crucial, and he labored under the assumption that Catholic teaching as it is mediated by the church's magisterium is normative. His entire project

---

[7] See Donald E. Pelotte, *John Courtney Murray: Theologian in Conflict* (New York: Paulist Press, 1975), 100.

consisted of demonstrating that what he proposed was faithful to and consistent with what had come before. Murray was also respectful of and obedient to the persons who had roles of authority over him. When he was ordered to stop publishing on religious liberty, he obeyed immediately, quickly returning to the university library all the books he had on the topic. He sought clarification from his superiors on exactly what he was and was not permitted to publish. He tried to break the impasse of his silencing through the publication of a new work on the topic in the journal most closely associated with the magisterium and requested that it first be specifically approved by the pope. And ultimately, he was vindicated and his teaching accepted by the Catholic magisterium at a highest level: an ecumenical council of the church.

But his story is also one by which "liberals" (or progressives, or whatever) can be inspired. Murray was a champion of personal conscience and freedom. He rejected the formulation of Catholic doctrine as it was offered and defended by those entrusted with its protection. He challenged the most powerful forces of the Vatican at a time when those forces wielded their power heavy handedly and, as it turned out in his case, wrongly. He was not content to simply repeat the same formulation of Catholic theology that had been passed down and defended by theologians and church teachers for many decades, even centuries.

What Is New Here

I'm not the first one to tell this story. It was told well in the 1976 book *John Courtney Murray: Theologian in Conflict*, by Donald E. Pelotte, SSS.[8] But Pelotte's book is now nearly forty years old, it is long out of print, and, having originated as a doctoral dissertation, it is also quite scholarly in approach. All of these factors make it, to some

---

[8] New York: Paulist Press, 1975. Two years after the book's publication, Pelotte was elected major superior of his order, the Congregation of the Blessed Sacrament, at the age of thirty-three. He went on to become the bishop of Gallup, New Mexico, a position he held from 1990 until his retirement in 2008. He was the first person of Native American decent to be named a bishop in the United States. Bishop Pelotte died in January 2010. See "Bishop emeritus of Gallup Donald E. Pelotte dies at 64," *Catholic News Agency*, January 8, 2010, http://www.catholicnewsagency.com/news /bishop_emeritus_of_gallup_donald_e._pelotte_dies_at_64/.

extent, somewhat inaccessible to many readers. Since its publication, various authors have looked at specific aspects of Murray's work and his story, most with a quite scholarly approach. But none have endeavored to tell the full story of his struggle to explore the truth about religious freedom.

Furthermore, many new resources have been published or made available that allow us to understand the story more fully, in a way that was simply impossible in 1976. Most especially:

- The multivolume *History of Vatican II*, edited by Giuseppe Alberigo and Joseph Komonchak and published in the United States by Orbis Books, provides a more thorough and complete picture of the preparations for and proceedings of the Second Vatican Council than was previously available.

- The church historian Joseph Komonchak has published valuable new research on the formal criticisms of Murray's work by the Holy Office (known today as the Congregation for the Doctrine of the Faith) and his silencing by Jesuit authorities under Vatican pressure. He has also unearthed new primary source material not previously available. This work of Komonchak's has, until now, been available in only somewhat obscure academic articles.

- The personal accounts of some key figures in this story have been made available. The personal journals of Fr. Joseph Clifford Fenton have been made available, most recently to a much wider audience via the internet, thanks to the efforts of The Catholic University of America's American Catholic Research Center and University Archives. The council diaries of Yves Congar have been published as well.

A Hell of a Story

I found myself thinking repeatedly throughout my work on this book: this is one hell of a story. For anyone who recognizes the importance of doctrine and theology, church and culture, government and human rights—any or all of the above—the narrative is both dramatic and important. It's a story that deserves retelling in our own day, half a century after the most dramatic events it includes.

Of course, there is little physical "action" going on here—no car chases or gun battles to be found—so it would be easy to dismiss it as an account of a bunch of scholars arguing in their academic journals about how many angels can fit on the head of a pin and old, celibate men getting together to decide what they think everyone else should believe. But that would miss the heart of it.

Make no mistake: this is a theological adventure story. It is about the adventure of humanity's encounter with God, God's revelation, and what that revelation means and doesn't mean to humankind. It's about the challenge of an institution and its leaders becoming too sure of knowing what God has said—using authority rather than reason to silence someone who suggests we look at it another way—but ultimately summoning the courage and the humility to listen to him, to consider the arguments, and to change.

A John Courtney Murray Timeline

September 12, 1904	Murray born in New York City
September 8, 1907	Pope Pius X publishes *Pascendi Dominici Gregis*
1920	Murray enters the Jesuit order
1927–1930	Murray teaches Latin and English literature at the Ateneo de Manila
1930–1934	Murray studies at Woodstock College, Maryland
June 25, 1933	Murray ordained a priest
1934–1937	Murray studies at Gregorian University, Rome
Fall 1937	Murray assigned to teach at Woodstock College
1941	Murray named editor-in-chief of *Theological Studies*
1943	Murray objects to Bishop McIntyre's refusal of permission to speak at Jewish Theological Seminary; McIntyre forwards correspondence to apostolic delegate to the United States
April 1945	Murray provides memo to Archbishop Mooney on religious freedom
June 1945	*Theological Studies* published first major Murray article on religious freedom

June 1948	Murray delivers major address to Catholic Theological Society of America on religious freedom; opposition from Francis Connell
May 1949	Paul Blanshard's *American Freedom and Catholic Power* published
June 1950	Henri de Lubac and other French Jesuits silenced
August 1950	Pope Pius XII's encyclical *Humani Generis* published
October 1950	Murray sends memo to Msgr. Montini on church-state relations in the United States
1951–1952	Murray serves as visiting professor of philosophy at Yale University
December 1952	*Theological Studies* publishes first of five articles on Pope Leo XIII's teaching on church-state relations and religious freedom
March 2, 1953	Cardinal Ottaviani delivers major address on church-state relations at Lateran University, criticizing Murray
April 1953	First Murray hospitalization due to cardiac problems
December 6, 1953	Pope Pius XII delivers *Ci Riesce* address to Catholic jurists
February 1954	Yves Congar and other French Dominicans silenced
March 25, 1954	Murray delivers address at The Catholic University of America on Pope Pius's *Ci Riesce*
April 1, 1954	Cardinal Ottaviani complains to Cardinal Spellman about Murray

Spring 1954	Publication of *The Catholic Church in World Affairs*, with Murray chapter on religious freedom
June 10, 1954	Joseph Fenton submits first report on Murray's work to Ottaviani
June 15, 1954	Fenton submits second report, on Murray and the American episcopate, to Ottaviani
July 7, 1954	Holy Office formally concludes review of Murray work, identifies four doctrinal errors, never makes it public
July 9, 1955	Jesuit officials inform Murray that sixth Leo XIII article forbidden from publication; Murray returns all books on the topic of religious freedom to library
October 9, 1958	Death of Pope Pius XII
October 28, 1958	Election of Pope John XXIII
January 25, 1959	Pope John XXIII announces plans for Vatican II
Fall 1960	Vatican II preparations begin in Rome, without Murray
Fall 1960	Publication of *We Hold These Truths*
December 12, 1960	Murray makes cover of *Time* magazine
October 11, 1962	Pope John XXIII convenes Vatican II session 1, Murray not present
December 8, 1962	Vatican II session 1 closes
February 11, 1963	Cardinal Spellman requests appointment of Murray as Vatican II *peritus*
Mid-February 1963	Murray banned from speaking on campus of The Catholic University of America

April 9, 1963	Murray informed of appointment as *peritus*
April 11, 1963	Publication of Pope John XXIII's encyclical *Pacem in Terris*
June 3, 1963	Death of Pope John XXIII
June 21, 1963	Election of Pope Paul VI
September 29, 1963	Vatican II session 2 opens, Murray present as *peritus*
November 12, 1963	Schema on religious freedom accepted, against Ottaviani objections, to be submitted for debate on the council floor
November 19, 1963	Bishop de Smedt introduces religious freedom Text 1 to council fathers
December 4, 1963	Vatican II session 2 closes
January 1964	Murray suffers first heart attack
September 14, 1964	Vatican II session 3 opens
September 23, 1964	Bishop de Smedt introduces religious freedom Text 2 to council fathers
September 23–25, 1964	Debate on the council floor on Text 2
October 9, 1964	Aborted attempt to introduce mixed commission on religious freedom schema
November 17, 1964	Council fathers receive religious freedom Text 3
November 19, 1964	"Black Thursday" on the council floor
November 21, 1964	Vatican II session 3 closes
December 1964	Murray suffers second heart attack
June 1965	Religious freedom Text 4 sent to council fathers around the world
September 14, 1965	Vatican II session 4 opens

September 15–22, 1965	Debate on Text 4 on council floor
October 5, 1965	Murray hospitalized with collapsed lung
October 25–27, 1965	Text 5 introduced to council fathers; debate takes place
November 17–19, 1965	Text 6 introduced to council fathers
November 18, 1965	Murray concelebrates Mass with Pope Paul VI
November 19, 1965	Council fathers vote in favor of Declaration on Religious Freedom
December 7, 1965	Declaration on Religious Freedom formally voted on by council fathers and proclaimed by Pope Paul VI as council document
December 8, 1965	Vatican II closes
May 1966	State of Massachusetts repeals ban on sale of contraception, following Murray's advising of Cardinal Cushing on the matter
Spring 1966	Murray honored with six honorary doctoral degrees
August 16, 1967	Murray suffers third heart attack, death in NYC taxi cab
July 7, 1969	Joseph Clifford Fenton dies
August 6, 1978	Pope Paul VI dies
August 3, 1979	Cardinal Ottaviani dies

Part One

Meet John Courtney Murray

Chapter 1

Who Is John Courtney Murray?

The year 1904 was a good one for the birth of theologians. John Courtney Murray was born that year, on September 12 in New York City. Within the same twelve-month period, at far-flung locations across the globe, several others who also would go on to become giants of Catholic theology were born: Karl Rahner in Germany in March, Yves Congar in France in April, and Bernard Lonergan in Canada that December.

The period of their birth was not, however, a great time for Catholic theology. Murray was born into a time when church leaders were engaged in heated battle with some of the most fundamental aspects of modernity, like individual freedoms and rights, democracy, conscience, and an attentiveness to the historical development of institutions and ideas. A loose collection of efforts by some Catholic scholars in Europe to integrate modern culture and thinking with the Gospel and theology was condemned as "modernism." In July 1907, the Vatican office known then as the Holy Inquisition (it would soon be renamed the Holy Office, and later, the Congregation for the Doctrine of the Faith) published a list of sixty-five modernist errors that it condemned. Then in September, Pope Pius X followed with his encyclical, *Pascendi Dominici Gregis*, "On the Doctrine of the Modernists." Condemning modernism as "the synthesis of all heresies," the pope insisted that it "means the destruction not of the Catholic religion alone, but of all religion." The pope called for strong remedies to root out modernist thinking. Catholic seminary and university teachers were to be investigated and anyone "found to be tainted with Modernism . . .

removed."[1] In 1910 came the Oath against Modernism, which all clergy were required to take annually until Pope Paul VI abrogated it in 1967. Also worth noting, given the work that lay ahead of Murray, is the publication in February 1906, less than eighteen months after his birth, of the encyclical *Vehementer Nos,* in which Pius X condemned the separation of church and state as "eminently disastrous and reprehensible."[2]

These powerful ecclesial currents would continue to flow into the years of Murray's adulthood. They would dramatically impact the course of his life and the content of his scholarly work. And like Lonergan, Congar, and Rahner, Murray would play a central role in reversing their flow.

First-Generation American

Murray's father, Michael John Murray, a Catholic, was an immigrant to the United States from Scotland early in life. He married Margaret Courtney, an immigrant from Ireland and also Catholic, and worked as an attorney in New York City. With their children John (whom the family called Jack), Katherine, and Elizabeth, they lived in Queens. Murray would remember his childhood as a happy and uneventful one. As the children of immigrants, Michael J. Schuck points out, the three Murray children surely grew up soaked in the same values as did millions of other first-generation Americans of their day: "inner strength, hard work, American freedom, and Catholic truth."[3]

Michael died in 1916, when John was twelve. Murray attended St. Francis Xavier High School, a Jesuit military academy, in Manhattan. Though he had thought for several years about being a doctor, he decided in 1920, at the age of sixteen, to enter the Jesuits.

[1] Pius X, encyclical letter *Pascendi Dominici Gregis,* http://www.vatican.va/holy _father/pius_x/encyclicals/documents/hf_p-x_enc_19070908_pascendi-dominici -gregis_en.html.

[2] Pius X, encyclical letter *Vehementer Nos,* http://www.vatican.va/holy_father /pius_x/encyclicals/documents/hf_p-x_enc_11021906_vehementer-nos_en.html.

[3] Michael J. Schuck, "John Courtney Murray's American Stories," in *Finding God in All Things: Celebrating Bernard Lonergan, John Courtney Murray, and Karl Rahner,* ed. Mark Bosco and David Stagaman (New York: Fordham University Press, 2007), 83–91, at 85.

Murray attended the then–newly opened Weston College, a Jesuit institution in Weston, Massachusetts (it would later be integrated into Boston College in 1959), where he earned his bachelor's degree in 1926 and master's degree in 1927. Following the traditional Jesuit course of formation for the time, Murray was sent in 1927 to teach Latin and English literature at the Ateneo de Manila in the Philippines.

In 1930 he returned to complete his studies at Woodstock College, the school of theology for Jesuits in their final years of formation, and was ordained a priest there on June 25, 1933, at the age of twenty-eight. He earned his license in sacred theology at Woodstock the following year and then was assigned to continue his studies at the Gregorian University in Rome. There he earned his doctorate in sacred theology in 1937 after completing a doctoral dissertation on Matthias Scheeben's theology of faith.

That same year, he was assigned to teach dogmatic theology (especially courses on grace and the Trinity) to the Jesuit seminarians at Woodstock, a post he would hold for the rest of his life. He was named editor-in-chief of the journal *Theological Studies* in 1941, another post he would hold until his death. Notably, he spent the 1951–1952 academic year as a visiting professor of philosophy at Yale University. For a Jesuit priest to teach at a university with such strong Protestant roots was highly unusual at the time.[4]

"Just Short of Awesome"

The most dominant aspect of Murray's personality was probably the air of urbane sophistication and erudition about him. Some were

[4] Early biographical details gathered from: Joseph A. Komonchak, "Murray, John Courtney," in *Encyclopedia of American Catholic History*, ed. Michael Glazier and Thomas J. Shelley (Collegeville, MN: Liturgical Press, 1997), 993–96; Mark Bosco, "Introduction," in Bosco and Stagaman, 6; Michael J. Schuck, "John Courtney Murray's American Stories," in Bosco and Stagaman, 83–91; Mark Williams, "Memories of 'Uncle Jack': A Nephew Remembers John Courtney Murray," in Bosco and Stagaman, 92–98, at 93; Thomas T. Love, *John Courtney Murray: Contemporary Church-State Theory* (Garden City, NY: Doubleday, 1965), 10; Douglas Auchincloss, "To Be Catholic and American," *Time* (December 12, 1960), http://content.time.com/time/subscriber/article/0,33009,871923,00.html.

impressed by it, while others took it as arrogance. His "thin and tower-ing" frame,[5] six feet four inches, only embellished these qualities. "Tall and imposing in appearance, he carried himself with a regal bearing that was just short of awesome," the journalist John Cogley wrote about him after his death.[6] Joseph Fenton, his staunchest intellectual adversary, wrote of Murray candidly in his personal journal, "He has a fine social presence. He speaks well. He has a certain arrogance which easily passes for culture and which seems to be the basis of his appeal."[7]

Murray was brilliant, and all those who knew him—admirers and foes alike—recognized it. It's the reason he was sent to the Gregorian University for further studies after ordination and the reason he was named editor-in-chief of *Theological Studies* at age thirty-seven. "God has given Fr. Murray a brilliant mind," wrote Francis Connell, another frequent critic of his theological work.[8] Still another, George Shea, acknowledged Murray's "impressive erudition, remarkable dexterity, and an uncommon command of language."[9]

The Dominican theologian Yves Congar, who worked closely with Murray during the council years, commented similarly in his own personal journal. After his first professional encounter with Murray in 1950, Congar commented on the "quite remarkable precision, quality, and intellectual rigor" of a paper Murray had delivered at an inter-national conference.[10] On one occasion during the council, Congar journaled, "Fr. Murray is less precise than I thought, and has no gift at

---

[5] "Religion: A Man of the City," *Time* (August 25, 1967), http://content.time.com/time/subscriber/article/0,33009,841042,00.html.

[6] John Cogley, "John Courtney Murray," *America* 117 (September 2, 1967): 220–21, at 221.

[7] Joseph Clifford Fenton, personal journal, "Ninth Trip to Rome, May 1954–June 1955," The American Catholic History Research Center and University Archives, The Catholic University of America, box 1, folder 3, available at http://doc.wrlc.org/handle/2041/112120. Hereafter, all citations from the personal journals of Joseph Clifford Fenton, held at CUA, will be cited as "Fenton journal," followed by more specific details.

[8] Francis J. Connell, "Reply to Father Murray," *American Ecclesiastical Review* 126 (January 1952): 49–59, at 58. Hereafter, *American Ecclesiastical Review* will be cited as *AER*.

[9] George W. Shea, "Catholic Doctrine and 'The Religion of the State,'" *AER* 123 (September 1950): 161–74, at 162.

[10] Cited in Joseph A. Komonchak, "'The Crisis in Church-State Relationships in the U.S.A.': A Recently Discovered Text by John Courtney Murray," *The Review of Politics* 61, no. 4 (Autumn 1999): 675–714, at 680.

all for elegant expressions. He is dry and brief."[11] On another occasion, though, he wrote that Murray "certainly has a welcome ability to make welcome the questions of others, which implies an interior humility and an authentic intellectual code of ethics. He also brings to his response a serenity characterized by a composure and a courteous distinction more British, even Oxonian, than American."[12] After the council had concluded, Congar wrote that Murray was "a true gentleman, with a sensational command of Latin!"[13]

Time magazine spoke of him in his 1960 cover article as "grave" and in his obituary as "long-faced to the point of looking sad."[14] But some who knew him personally recognized a warmer side of Murray. A journalist spoke of him after his death as "a warm and totally enjoyable human being."[15] The same writer reported the delightful memories that his peers recounted at length about Murray when they gathered after his funeral. His nephew would remember, decades after his death, his "warm and loving smile" and his "mirthfulness and lightness of spirit."[16] More than one person would remember being admonished by him, "Courage! It's far more important than intelligence."[17]

Murray suffered from persistent poor health throughout his adult life. He had chronic back pain and acute bursitis that was the result of a club foot at the end of his right leg. By the last decade of his life, his back pain was often debilitating; there were times he was unable to genuflect at Mass and bowed only with great difficulty.[18]

---

[11] Yves Congar, *My Journal of the Council* (Collegeville, MN: Liturgical Press, 2012), 731.

[12] Ibid., 736.

[13] Ibid., 893.

[14] "Religion: A Man of the City."

[15] John Cogley, "John Courtney Murray," *America* 117 (September 2, 1967): 220–21, at 221.

[16] Williams, "Memories of 'Uncle Jack,'" in Bosco and Stagaman, 92.

[17] Walter Burghart cited the statement in the homily he preached at Murray's funeral (quoted by Richard John Neuhaus in "Democracy, Desperately Dry," in *John Courtney Murray and the American Civil Conversation*, ed. Robert P. Hunt and Kenneth L. Grasso [Grand Rapids, MI: Eerdmans, 1992], 3–18, at 8), and Murray's nephew recalled the same phrase decades after Murray's death (Williams, "Memories of 'Uncle Jack,'" in Bosco and Stagaman, 94).

[18] Williams, "Memories of 'Uncle Jack,'" in Bosco and Stagaman, 94.

He also suffered for years with a heart condition. He was first hospitalized with heart problems in April 1953. His first heart attack came in January 1964, and a second one followed in December of the same year. He was hospitalized again in October 1965 with a collapsed lung. His third heart attack, just before his sixty-third birthday, took his life in a New York City taxi cab on August 16, 1967.

Murray's Achievements

Though Murray is today best known for his 1960 book *We Hold These Truths: Catholic Reflections on the American Proposition*, a collection of previously published articles on the topic of public theology, it is neither his best nor his most significant work. His finest and most consequential work falls specifically in the area of religious freedom. He did this through a large body of scholarly articles on the topic published largely in theological journals and through his work at the Second Vatican Council.

As will be explained in the pages that follow, Murray made enormous contributions to the topic by bringing to light new insights and new understandings of the historical context of the Catholic Church's previous teaching on the topic, and he did it in spite of opposition from some of the most powerful and influential figures within the church of his day. Though he never wrote a book on the topic, he published thirty-eight articles on it before the council began 1962, then another thirty during and after the council. In all, sixty-eight of his 166 published articles were on religious freedom.[19]

These contributions had great influence on the bishops gathered at the Second Vatican Council, especially the American bishops, and contributed mightily to the production and promulgation of *Dignitatis Humanae*, the council's Declaration on Religious Freedom (1965). The document marked a dramatic and historic shift in the teaching of the Church's universal magisterium. It also influenced in powerful ways both the teaching of future church leaders (witness Pope John

[19] J. Leon Hooper, "General Introduction," in John Courtney Murray, *Religious Liberty: Catholic Struggles with Pluralism* (Louisville, KY: Westminster/John Knox Press, 1993), 12, 27.

Paul II's vibrant defense of religious freedom throughout the world in the latter decades of the twentieth century) and also the ministry and social engagement of Catholics working, sometimes quite effectively, to transform diverse parts of human society.

Chapter 2

The "Received Opinion"

To most people in the West today, it seems obvious: everyone has the right to choose his or her religious faith freely and to worship publicly, without coercion or impediment by any law or government. But in 1950, to almost any Catholic prelate or theologian, and certainly to those at the Vatican, this was far from obvious. To understand the drama of what John Courtney Murray proposed and why it appeared not only mistaken but also threatening and heretical to many, you have to realize where things stood on the topic when Murray took it up.

The drama is grounded firmly in the context of what has sometimes been called "the long nineteenth century"—that is, the period stretching from the start of the French Revolution in 1789 to the onset of the First World War in 1914, during which the church and society were primarily engaged in reacting to and assimilating the French Revolution's meaning. The entire period was marked by an ongoing war between the papacy and the modern world, with the papacy suffering repeated setbacks in battle after battle, even while voicing occasional cries of victory, however futile.

The Long Nineteenth Century

Throughout the Middle Ages, the church had dominated European life. It provided order and nurtured a livable and humane society, founded on tradition, authority, and the divine revelation that it interpreted and guarded. The period of the Enlightenment—marked at least as much by a new *attitude* about the world and human existence as by particular events or achievements—challenged that dominance.

No longer could tradition and traditional authority be relied on as the surest touchstones of life. These were replaced by reason, knowledge, and liberty.

The superstars of the Enlightenment were writers like Diderot, whose remarkable *Encyclopédie* purported to catalog all human knowledge; Montesquieu, who advocated a government of distinct legislative, executive, and judicial branches, each bound by the rule of law; and Voltaire, whose sharp essays skewered dogmatism, religious intolerance, and, most especially, the Catholic Church. These writers' ideas shook the foundations of European society and questioned everything that the church was perceived to represent.

Beginning in 1789, the Enlightenment found violent and at times chaotic expression in the French Revolution, a popular overthrow of the *ancien regime* (the "old order," in which the church had played a central role) in the name of liberty, equality, and fraternity. The church was a central and constant target of the Revolution from the start. Church property was nationalized, convents were closed, and clergy were forced to take an oath of loyalty to the new constitution. A new calendar that did not count years from the birth of Christ was adopted, and one writer of the time famously looked forward to the time when the last king would be strangled with the entrails of the last priest.[1] The Vatican reacted to these attacks and affronts with a quick and forceful rejection of everything associated with the Revolution, including the Declaration of the Rights of Man produced by the French assembly (with some cooperation from Thomas Jefferson) in August 1789.

The Revolution's assault on the church continued with the reign of Napoleon Bonaparte, who represented its ideals. Bonaparte's army took the Papal States and occupied Rome in 1798, taking the pope captive. The Papal States were soon restored but fell again and were restored again in the following years.

Despite all this, some Catholic thinkers tried to forge a positive relationship between Catholicism and liberalism. The priest Félicité Robert de Lamennais, for example, produced important writings that explained how freedom of the press, religious freedom, and the

---

[1] See *The Oxford Dictionary of Quotations*, 4th ed. rev., ed. Angela Partington (New York: Oxford University Press, 1996), 458.

separation of church and state were consistent with Catholic tradition. Pope Gregory XVI's 1832 encyclical *Mirari Vos* rebuked such efforts. In the document, the pope fretted about the "evil and dangerous times" the church faced, condemned freedom of conscience as "absurd," and branded those who supported a separation of church and state as "shameless lovers of liberty."[2]

The door to hopes of conciliation between Catholicism and modernity during that era slammed shut in 1864 with the publication of Pope Pius IX's encyclical *Quanta Cura* and its more famous appendix, *The Syllabus of Errors*. The latter was a terse list of eighty errors of the modern world. Included among them were the separation of church and state and religious freedom. It concluded by condemning the notion that "the Roman Pontiff can, and ought to, reconcile himself, and come to terms with, progress, liberalism, and modern civilization."[3]

With the loss of the Papal States again (this time permanently) in 1870, the hierarchy saw itself, and therefore the whole church, as being under siege by the modern world. Pope Pius IX dramatically declared himself to be a "prisoner in the Vatican," refusing not only to leave Vatican property but also even to appear in the balcony of Saint Peter's Basilica overlooking its square. Rather than delivering the annual New Year's blessing on the world from that balcony, as was tradition, he delivered it instead from a courtyard balcony within the Vatican, unseen by the public. The "prisoner in the Vatican" stance (which persisted until 1929, when the Lateran Treaty created Vatican City State) is a good expression of the relationship that the church understood itself to have with the modern world: separate, on guard, closed off. (Perhaps not coincidentally, 1870 was also the year that the First Vatican Council proclaimed the dogma of papal infallibility.)

The long nineteenth century labored on. In the 1870s, Otto von Bismarck tried to root the church out of Prussian society. The year 1905 brought a radical separation of church and state in France. In stubborn opposition, Pope Pius XI proclaimed the feast of Christ the King in

[2] Gregory XVI, encyclical letter *Mirari Vos* (1832), http://www.papalencyclicals.net/Greg16/g16mirar.htm.

[3] Pius IX, *Syllabus of Errors*, http://www.papalencyclicals.net/Pius09/p9syll.htm.

1925, insisting that no matter what any society or leader thought, Jesus Christ is truly the king of every place.

"Only Our Religion Has the Right to Exist"

But if the church rejected religious freedom and insisted that a government's refusal to formally recognize and protect the church and participate in its worship of God was a grave sin, what were the millions of Catholics who lived in Western nations to do? Could they participate in civic life at all? Did the church's stance not suggest that to hold positions in government at any level, to vote, or to pledge allegiance to such a nation's constitution meant cooperating in an evil system? Didn't this stance logically call for civil disobedience on the part of Catholics in many countries?

A less dramatic solution was offered by Bishop Felix Dupanloup, a prominent leader of the church in France in the mid-1800s. Dupanloup theorized that in an ideal situation, a government would indeed declare it and its nation to be Catholic; it would support and defend the Catholic faith; its leaders would worship in an official capacity as Catholics; and it would prevent public worship by non-Catholics from taking place. But, he said, in the modern world, this was simply not going to happen in many cases; for the church to insist on it would be unrealistic, impractical, and could even bring negative consequences upon itself. To avoid such consequences, Catholics could morally accept, cooperate with, and make accommodations to the historical circumstances. Borrowing some medieval vocabulary,[4] Dupanloup called the ideal situation the *thesis*, while the historical circumstances to be accommodated were the *hypothesis*. When he offered this explanation in

---

[4] The philosopher Boethius (ca. AD 475–526) had used the words *thesis* and *hypothesis* to describe the difference between the two forms of communication, dialectic and rhetoric. Dialectic, he said, is concerned with what is universally true, regardless of circumstances. It uses careful logic and rigid syllogisms to make the truth clear even to those who do not wish to accept it. The matter of dialectic is thesis. Rhetoric, on the other hand, takes account of the circumstances in which it works. It uses approximations to persuade the listener. The matter of rhetoric is hypothesis. See Richard McKeon, "Rhetoric in the Middle Ages," *Speculum* 17, no. 1 (January 1942): 1–32, at 10–11.

a brochure he published in 1885, Dupanloup quickly received letters of thanks from the pope and from hundreds of other bishops in Europe.[5]

Bishop Dupanloup's theory was widely embraced in the church. Though official papal documents of the following century rarely adopted his terminology, they certainly presumed it. In 1895, for example, Pope Leo XIII wrote an encyclical letter to the American bishops "On Catholicism in the United States." Leo praised the rapid social and economic development that had taken place in the United States over the previous century and the impressive growth of Catholic parishes and institutions. He acknowledged gratefully that the church in America was able to flourish "unopposed by the Constitution and government of your nation, fettered by no hostile legislation, protected against violence by the common laws and the impartiality of the tribunals." But, the pope continued,

> though all this is true, it would be very erroneous to draw the conclusion that in America is to be sought the type of the most desirable status of the Church, or that it would be universally lawful or expedient for State and Church to be, as in America, dissevered and divorced. The fact that Catholicity with you is in good condition, nay, is even enjoying a prosperous growth, is by all means to be attributed to the fecundity with which God has endowed His Church, in virtue of which unless men or circumstances interfere, she spontaneously expands and propagates herself; but she would bring forth more abundant fruits if, in addition to liberty, she enjoyed the favor of the laws and the patronage of the public authority.[6]

In other words, things were indeed going well for the church in the United States and the Vatican could live with the present church-state

---

[5] Dominique Gonnet, *La Liberté Religieuse à Vatican II: La contribution de John Courtney Murray, SJ* (Paris: Editions du Cerf, 1994), 31–32; William L. Portier, "Theology of Manners as Theology of Containment: John Courtney Murray and *Dignitatis Humanae* Forty Years After," *U.S. Catholic Historian* 24, no. 1 (Winter 2006): 83–105, at 85.

[6] Leo XIII, encyclical letter *Longinqua* (1895), http://www.vatican.va/holy_father/leo_xiii/encyclicals/documents/hf_l-xiii_enc_06011895_longinqua_en.html.

arrangements there, since it had to anyway; but no one ought to think that things would not be going even better if the arrangements were as they ought to be: a Catholic American government guiding a Catholic American nation.

That is where the matter stood in Catholic theology, right up to the time Murray turned to the question in the 1940s. For example, an April 1948 article published in the journal *La Civiltà Cattolica* puts it this way:

> The Roman Catholic Church, convinced, through its divine prerogatives, of being the only true Church, must demand the right to freedom for herself alone, because such a right can only be possessed by truth, never by error. As to other religions, the Church will certainly never draw the sword, but she will require that by legitimate means they shall not be allowed to propagate false doctrine. Consequently, in a State where the majority of the people are Catholic, the Church will require that legal existence be denied to error, and that if religious minorities actually exist, they shall have only a de facto existence, without opportunity to spread their beliefs. If, however, actual circumstances . . . make the complete application of this principle impossible, then the Church will require for herself all possible concessions. . . . We ask Protestants to understand that the Catholic Church would betray her trust if she were to proclaim . . . that error can have the same rights as truth. . . . The Church cannot blush for her own want of tolerance, as she asserts it in principle and applies it in practice.[7]

Just a few years earlier, theologian Francis Connell (who will play a significant role in Murray's story), put the matter even more bluntly:

> One form of religion has been made obligatory on all mankind by the Son of God under penalty of eternal damnation and . . . no other form of religion has any right

---

[7] Fiorello Cavalli, "La Condizione dei Protestanti in Spagna," *La Civilà Cattolica* 2 (April 1948): 29–47; English translation quoted in W. Russell Bowie, "Protestant Concern over Catholicism," *American Mercury* 69 (September 1949): 261–73, at 264.

> by divine law to exist or to propagate. . . . Ours is the
> only religion that has the right to exist, and . . . the
> existence of any non-Catholic denomination is opposed to the
> plan of God's providence for mankind.[8]

These are not the unfortunate statements of people with an elementary grasp of Catholic doctrine. All the contents of *La Civiltà Cattolica* were approved by the Vatican secretary of state's office prior to publication, and Connell was a highly regarded professor of theology at The Catholic University of America.[9] A few years later, some of the church's most prominent leaders expressed the same thinking during the deliberations of the Second Vatican Council.

A typical shorthand was to speak of the church's dual endorsement of "dogmatic intolerance and personal tolerance." That is, Catholics had to be aware that people and society really had no objective right not to be Catholic or to believe what was not true, but subjectively, Catholics could and should tolerate the fact that there were non-Catholics around them.

Very Real Consequences

This was no purely theoretical exercise. For many decades the popes and their diplomats worked diligently, sometimes with real success, to establish concordats (diplomatic agreements) that established in the laws of nations the principles of the thesis-hypothesis approach.

An 1862 concordat between Pope Pius IX and the Republic of Ecuador decreed that only Catholics could be citizens of the nation or had rights, positions that were written into the nation's constitution a few years later.[10] In Italy, the Lateran Pacts of 1929 affirmed Cathol-

[8] Francis J. Connell, "Catholics and 'Interfaith' Groups," *AER* 105 (November 1941): 337–53, at 347, 353.

[9] For other contemporary expressions of this approach, see Joseph Clifford Fenton, "The Status of the Controversy," *AER* 124 (June 1951): 327–52; Fenton, "Principles Underlying Traditional Church-State Doctrine," *AER* 126 (June 1952): 452–62; Maurice Bévenot, "Thesis and Hypothesis," *Theological Studies* 15 (1954): 440–46.

[10] See "Concordat between Pope Pius IX and the Republic of Ecuador (1862)," Concordat Watch, http://www.concordatwatch.eu/showtopic.php?org_id=40037&kb_header_id=47262.

icism as the state religion (a situation that lasted until 1984). Similar concordats were negotiated with Portugal in 1940, Spain in 1953, and the Dominican Republic in 1954. These agreements typically outlawed public worship by non-Catholic groups and gave the church wide authority in the censorship of publications and in public education.

The thesis-hypothesis framework was widely understood in the church as official Catholic teaching. John Courtney Murray would insist repeatedly that it was not. It did not, he argued, represent the unchangeable and universal core of Catholic doctrine. He called it, rather, "the received opinion." And he would argue that the received opinion, in contemporary circumstances, "[ought] not to be received."[11]

[11] John Courtney Murray, "Notes from which Fr. Murray spoke in McMahon Hall, Catholic University, March 25, 1954," The Reverend John Courtney Murray, SJ, Papers, Georgetown University Special Collections Research Center, Series 4, box 5, folder 402.

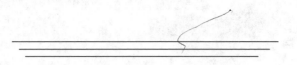

Part Two

Battle Lines

Chapter 3

Intercredal Cooperation
(1942–1945)

In August 1940, during the height of Adolf Hitler's air war against Great Britain, Cardinal Arthur Hinsley, the Roman Catholic archbishop of Westminster, launched a movement that he called "the Sword of the Spirit." In a special radio broadcast, Hinsley said he hoped to help Catholics understand, in the midst of social and international chaos, the social teachings of their church and the important ways it could shape not only the daily lives of individuals but also politics and international relations. Through prayer, study, and action, Sword of the Spirit members would develop a Christian way of looking at social issues and "bring back the idea of God and the idea of Morality into every field of human activity, national and international, politics, business, private life, education."[1]

Unexpected Ecumenism

Offering a religious message with a strong anti-Nazi, nationalistic flavor at a time of national crisis, the effort quickly saw widespread success. The movement's activities included mass gatherings led by prominent prelates, smaller community gatherings, and parish study groups. Two years after its launch, well-known Catholic writer Frank Sheed could write that the Sword of the Spirit had been "welcomed

---

[1] F. J. Sheed, "The Sword of the Spirit," *The Ecclesiastical Review* 107, no. 2 (August 1942): 81–92, at 83, quoting from a contemporary periodical published by the movement.

everywhere with a spontaneity which has greeted no other movement launched by a Catholic in modern England. Its first notable spread was in the armed forces . . . but Catholics all over England were also rallying to it. . . . The Movement spread at an incredible speed."[2]

Unexpectedly, Sword of the Spirit activities received intense interest from Anglicans and other non-Catholics. Many began attending its public meetings and participating in study groups that met at Catholic parishes. If that does not seem particularly noteworthy today, it was a startling development in the early 1940s.

Cardinal Hinsley welcomed and encouraged this development. The London *Times* published a letter he cosigned with the two Anglican archbishops in England and the moderator of the Free Church Federal Council. Together they called for the abolition of "extreme inequality in wealth and possessions," broader access to educational opportunities for children, more efforts to promote the well-being of families, restoration of "the sense of a Divine vocation" in all that people do, and equitable access to and wise use of the earth's resources.[3] These same leaders, along with other prominent figures, participated in large Sword of the Spirit events around the nation.

Not everyone was enthusiastic about this development, and soon church leaders and scholars, both Catholic and Protestant, were hotly debating "intercredal cooperation"—the term that developed for Christians of different churches or believers of different religions working together for the good of society. Some Catholics suggested that such activities would promote "indifferentism," the impression that one faith is as good as another, or that the differences between Catholic doctrine and that of other churches were minimal. One prominent scholar insisted in the April 1942 issue of *The Clergy Review* that there could be between Catholics and Protestants no collective worship, no efforts toward ecclesial reunion, no discussions or activities that might encourage fundamentalism or indifferentism on the part of Catholics—indeed, *no* cooperation on a "so-called Christian basis," since no such basis existed. "It is sometimes said," the author wrote, "that Catholics

[2] Ibid., 81.
[3] Ibid., 89–90.

and Protestants have Charity in common. But their Charity is not our Charity. The words are the same but the content is different."[4]

Cardinal Hinsley acknowledged the danger of indifferentism, but he insisted that the movement's leaders took many precautions to avoid it and that the risks were well worth the important potential benefits to society. "We are too small a body by ourselves to influence the social order," Hinsley said, "so the only alternatives which face us are either to cooperate with other Christians or to abandon altogether the social order to the atheists and secularists who have already done it such appalling harm."[5]

But by April 1942, largely due to the controversy, Anglican and Free Church participants had set up a parallel organization, the Religion and Life Movement. The two movements were linked by a joint committee and frequently held joint meetings and formal discussions on social issues. The two organizations sometimes ran parallel multi-day programs in the same community at the same time, with the same structure and activities going on at each, both culminating in a single joint meeting.[6]

Interest in these ecumenical activities soon reached other European countries and the United States. In the United States, interfaith or "three-faith" (Catholic, Protestant, and Jewish) meetings and organizations, such as the Council against Intolerance in America and the Greater New York Interfaith Committee, appeared. The National Conference of Christians and Jews sponsored thousands of "trialogue" events—where three-person teams of a Catholic, a Protestant, and a Jew (often a priest, minister, and rabbi) sat together on stage to discuss

[4] William Butterfield, "Co-operation with Non-Catholics," *The Clergy Review* 22 (April 1942): 160–65.

[5] Michael J. Walsh, "Ecumenism in War-time Britain: The Sword of the Spirit and Religion and Life, 1940–1945 (I)," *The Heythrop Journal* 23, no. 3 (July 1982): 243–58, at 252; Sheed, "The Sword of the Spirit," 91, citing a quotation in a Sword of the Spirit publication.

[6] Barbara Ward, "'Sword of the Spirit' Crusade Is a Clear Call Out of Chaos," *America* 67 (August 29, 1942): 566–67; Walsh, "Ecumenism . . . (I)," 258; Michael J. Walsh, "Ecumenism in War-time Britain: The Sword of the Spirit and Religion and Life, 1940–1945 (II)," *The Heythrop Journal* 23, no. 4 (October 1982): 377–394, at 383.

their religious beliefs before an audience—in schools, churches, and libraries around the country.[7]

Catholic supporters of all this found encouragement from papal teaching of the previous century calling for joint action by Catholics and non-Catholics in the interests of social harmony, peace between nations, and a society more thoroughly imbued with religious values.[8] But as in Britain, not everyone cheered.

An early critic in the United States was Fr. Francis Connell, a Redemptorist priest, prolific writer, and professor of moral theology at The Catholic University of America. In a November 1941 article in the *Ecclesiastical Review* (the journal would soon be renamed the *American Ecclesiastical Review* and have an ongoing and significant place in Murray's story), Connell acknowledged the importance of Catholics relating charitably to their non-Catholic neighbors and called the new, cooperative spirit "a blessing." But he warned of the danger of charitable behavior fostering indifferentism. Though Catholics could respect the sincerity of people of other creeds, he said, "we cannot appreciate or respect or honor their doctrinal differences from the Catholic creed."[9]

For an ordinary Catholic to discuss his or her faith with a member of a different church, Connell said, brought serious "spiritual dangers," while frequent association with non-Catholics brought the further risk of mixed marriages. A Catholic was permitted to speak in public to explain the Church's doctrines, but events of a religious nature where a Catholic stood on equal footing with a Protestant were forbidden by canon law. Connell wrote, "When simple people, who are inclined to identify individuals with the cause they represent, see their priest recognizing the clergymen of other creeds as his equals at such gatherings, they are liable to conclude that he regards their religions as equal to his, or at least that he considers difference of belief as unimportant."[10]

---

[7] See Francis J. Connell, "Catholics and 'Interfaith' Groups," *The Ecclesiastical Review* 105 (November 1941): 337–53, at 341, 346.

[8] See Wilfrid Parsons, "Intercredal Co-operation in the Papal Documents," *Theological Studies* 4 (June 1943): 159–82.

[9] Connell, "Catholics and 'Interfaith' Groups," 340, 346.

[10] Ibid., 349.

Even the words being used to describe these meetings—"interfaith" or "three-faith"—were inappropriate, Connell said, because "there is only one real faith." He insisted the meetings and organizations were "a grave menace to the faith of our people" and concluded, "Whatever good they may be producing is far outweighed by their disastrous spiritual consequences."[11]

"Social Unity or Destruction"

As a lively discussion played out on the pages of several Catholic journals, Fr. John Courtney Murray, SJ, stepped into the fray. Working at the time as both the editor of the new journal *Theological Studies* and the culture editor at *America* magazine, Murray had studied in Europe during the 1930s and seen the turmoil caused there by the Depression, the collapse of democracy and rise of totalitarianism, and the war in Spain. As a result, he saw intercredal cooperation as an important development for the times.

Between September 1942 and June 1943, Murray published a series of three articles on the controversy in *Theological Studies*. He praised the movement's "freshness and victorious spirit"[12] and warned of Western society's ever-growing secularization as a major threat to the moral and spiritual well-being of individuals and families that demanded cooperative resistance by people of different religions. What was needed, he wrote, was "a respiritualization of the whole ethos of society" or, more concretely, the creation of "a new set of social institutions that will exert a permanent pressure on the social conscience in the direction of high domestic morality."[13]

Murray wrote:

> This work [of intercredal cooperation] is the creation of a new complex of ethical currents in society, and their incorporation in a new set of social institutions, in order that both together

---

[11] Ibid.

[12] John Courtney Murray, "Current Theology: Christian Co-operation," *Theological Studies* 3 (September 1942): 413–31, at 431.

[13] John Courtney Murray, "Current Theology: Intercredal Co-operation: Its Theory and Its Organization," *Theological Studies* 4 (June 1943): 257–86, at 258, 262.

may support, instead of crushing, the moral conscience as well as the temporal happiness of mankind. . . . Whether we like it or not, we are living in a religiously pluralist society at a time of spiritual crisis; and the alternatives are the discovery of social unity, or destruction.[14]

To Murray, intercredal cooperation was "based on the essence of Catholicism," because it was thoroughly incarnational, recognizing and being willing to build on the working of grace not just inside the church but in human nature.[15] He did not ignore the objections raised by others, and he acknowledged the danger of fostering indifferentism. But he suggested that those who objected (mentioning Connell by name) had failed to consider the danger that Catholics faced along with believers of other faiths if they did not confront secularism together. Murray argued that an ambitious program of doctrinal instruction for Catholics, focusing especially on "the mission of the church in the temporal order," would decrease the threat of indifferentism.[16]

Murray noted repeatedly that several popes had encouraged cooperation of Catholics with others in society. Especially relevant and compelling for him was the judgment of Pope Pius IX, who had said in the encyclical *Singulari Quadam* that German Catholics might licitly join trade unions that were not explicitly Catholic when it was for the purpose of securing workers' rights and generally improving social conditions.[17] Noting that the pope saw intercredal cooperation as important in confronting "powerful social movements of an anti-religious character,"[18] Murray wrote:

> My point, therefore, is that the present-day discussion of inter-credal co-operation must be guided by the profoundly Catholic doctrine underlying the *Singulari Quadam*, as well as by its particular phrases. It is again a problem of balance, of finding the center, and of avoiding the temptation to be drawn to one

---

[14] Ibid., 262, 274. See also John Courtney Murray, "Reversing the Secularist Drift," *Thought* 24 (March 1949): 36–46.

[15] Murray, "Current Theology: Intercredal Co-operation," 274–75.

[16] Murray, "Current Theology: Christian Co-operation," 416.

[17] Murray, "Current Theology: Intercredal Co-operation," 263–72.

[18] Ibid., 272.

pole of the tension. Rome, of course, is in the center. And, if
I mistake not, the significant thing today is that Rome has, so
to speak, moved the center to the left.[19]

In October 1943, Francis Connell responded with an article in
the *Ecclesiastical Review*. Faithfully offering the thesis-hypothesis approach, he warned against the idea, increasingly popular in the United
States, that all people have the right to choose and practice whatever
religion most appeals to them. "No Catholic can in conscience defend
such an idea," he wrote, for Catholicism is "the only religion that has a
genuine right to exist." Allowing that a person who sincerely believed
their conscience led them to practice a religion other than Catholicism
was bound by that very fact to do so, Connell said that "this subjective
obligation, based on an erroneous conscience, does not give him a genuine right. A real right is something objective, based on truth." For that
reason, Connell said, "a Catholic government has the right, absolutely
speaking, to restrict the activities of non-Catholic denominations, in
order to protect the Catholic citizens from spiritual harm."[20]

To Connell, it was fine for faithful Catholics to acknowledge that
US law granted all people the right to choose their religion. But they
had to understand that God did not.[21]

First Official Concerns

Before concluding this chapter, we should note that it was during
this period that Murray had his first run-in with ecclesiastical authority.
In 1943, he was invited to lecture at the Institute for Religious Studies
at Jewish Theological Seminary in New York on the challenges facing
the church. Wishing to accept the invitation, he asked the permission
of Bishop Francis McIntyre, the vicar general of the Archdiocese of
New York (and later the cardinal archbishop of Los Angeles). When
McIntyre denied the permission, Murray responded with a letter to
him that vigorously defended his positions.

[19] Ibid., 271.
[20] Francis J. Connell, "Pope Leo XIII's Message to America," *The Ecclesiastical
Review* 109 (October 1943): 249–56, at 255.
[21] Ibid.

McIntyre promptly forwarded copies of the correspondence to the Vatican's Apostolic Delegate to the United States, Archbishop Amleto Cicognani. But there is no record of what, if anything, Cicognani did with the letters.[22]

---

[22] Joseph A. Komonchak, "The Silencing of John Courtney Murray," in *Cristianesimo nella Storia: Saggi in Onore di Giuseppe Alberigo*, ed. A. Melloni, et al. (Bologna: Il Mulino, 1996), 657–702, at 658–59.

Chapter 4

The Conversation Turns: Religious Freedom
(1945–1948)

During World War II, President Roosevelt identified "Four Freedoms" for which the Allies were fighting and to which every person had a right: freedom of speech, freedom of worship, freedom from want, and freedom from fear. The concept was enthusiastically embraced across the nation, a fact perhaps best expressed by the famous set of four paintings by Norman Rockwell, originally published in the *Saturday Evening Post* in 1943. By the spring of 1945, the war was clearly nearing its end and a strong movement was developing in favor of an internationally recognized statement of rights that all human beings possess. So religious freedom was very much a topic that was "on the table" in both politics and popular culture. Murray's interest in intercredal cooperation soon led him to this obviously related issue.

An Initial Approach Abandoned

In a March 1945 article in *Theological Studies*, Murray assessed the work of the Federal Council of Churches' Joint Committee on Religious Liberty, formed three years earlier. Comprised of thirteen Protestant scholars and leaders and headed by the president of Princeton, the group had composed a Statement on Religious Liberty and presented it to the US president, secretary of state, and all members of congress. One of the group's scholars was preparing a book on the

29

topic. "It is evident," Murray wrote, "that religious liberty is a political problem of the first magnitude."[1]

Murray was critical of the group's statement, though most of his criticism was directed at the method and reasoning it employed. He said it conceived the right to religious liberty "in the typically Protestant atomistic way," included several examples of defective logic, and failed to provide a theory to support the rights it asserted.[2]

Murray wrote that it was time for the Catholic Church to offer a "pacific and full exposition of our own theory of religious liberty." He noted that Catholic teaching on the topic was commonly perceived as "purely opportunistic" and said this was largely because it was misunderstood.[3] He closed with a promise of a more thorough exploration of the subject in a later article, noting three important aspects of the problem that would need to be considered: ethical, theological, and political.

Impressed by the article, Archbishop Edward Mooney of Detroit approached Murray to request his participation in a meeting with the Federal Council of Churches. He apparently asked for further exposition of religious freedom from Murray, because Murray provided Mooney with a lengthy memo on the topic. Dated April 1945, it is eighteen typewritten, mostly single-spaced, pages long. He repeated his assertion that the problem needed to be approached on three levels: ethical, theological, and political.[4]

In June 1945, Murray published a major article in *Theological Studies*, fleshing out the same ideas found in the section of his Mooney memo on the ethical aspect of the question and suggesting that further installments would consider the issue's theological and political elements.[5] But the promised second and third articles never appeared. The

---

[1] John Courtney Murray "Current Theology: Freedom of Religion," *Theological Studies* 6 (March 1945): 85–113, at 87.

[2] Ibid., 94.

[3] Ibid., 89–90.

[4] John Courtney Murray, "Notes on the Theory of Religious Liberty," *April 1945 Memo to Archbishop Edward Mooney*, Georgetown University Library, Special Collections Research Center, John Courtney Murray Papers, box 7, file 555.

[5] John Courtney Murray, "Freedom of Religion, I: The Ethical Problem," *Theological Studies* 6 (June 1945): 229–86, at 234–35. (Of course, the "I" in the title clearly suggests this, too.)

Mooney memo and the June 1945 *Theological Studies* article together offer a helpful picture of Murray's thinking at that point in time.

A "Natural and Necessary" Union

What is clear is that in the spring of 1945, at the age of forty, Murray's thinking on religious freedom reflected in most respects the commonly accepted Catholic approach to the topic. It was an approach he would very shortly move beyond, and in doing so, he would meet great opposition.

Murray approached the topic by considering what the individual person owes, in conscience, to God and the state and what the state owes to God and to the consciences of individuals. The individual owes God the search for truth, the act of worship, the development of a well-formed conscience, the fostering of the well-being of family and civil society, and the helping of others to know and obey God better. To the state, the individual owes the fostering of a healthy society, the building up of strong and just institutions within society, and respect for public authority and laws.[6]

Regarding what the state owes to God, Murray wrote that it is obliged "to acknowledge God as its author, to worship Him as He wills to be worshipped, and to subject its official life and action to His law." It must therefore promote religion and morality and can never be neutral toward "errors and evils that affect the social order." It "has no right to act as if there were no God. . . . It is, therefore, morally obliged to assume the position that atheism and actions contrary to the natural law have no rights in the social order, and that they can claim no freedom of public advocacy or practice." Indeed, the state has "the right to restrict the propaganda of atheism or secularism and the practice of immorality." While the state always has these rights, it may choose not to exercise them for reasons of prudence, when the common good would be better served by not exercising them.[7]

Murray said that when a state's authority is in conflict with God's authority, citizens are internally and unjustly divided between the two. For the good of the citizen's integrity and peace, the state must support

---

[6] Ibid., 263–66.
[7] Ibid., 266–69.

the law of God. It is therefore subject to it. He calls this "the essential preliminary step" toward understanding the church-state question and "the ethical substratum" of the church's teaching on it.[8] To Archbishop Mooney, Murray wrote, "This is the key to the Catholic doctrine with regard to the ideal solution of the problem of religious liberty: the juridical union of Church and State is the natural and necessary consequence of the vital union of the Christian and citizen in the one man." The "ordered connection" between the spiritual and public lives of people called for a corresponding connection between church and state.[9]

Murray said this arrangement had never been perfectly realized in concrete historical circumstances and never would. Noting that the government would need to be run by Christians for this arrangement to work, he wrote, "It is, for instance, unthinkable that the Church would consider union of Church and State desirable in Turkey, or in Egypt, or even in the United States, at the present moment."[10] Therefore, union of church and state is not always the best solution in a given situation.

Regarding the separation of church and state, Murray said there was a difference between the act of separation where it previously had not existed and a long-standing state of being separated in places like the United States. Where the separation ensures social peace, the church can tolerate it. Murray acknowledged that this position was commonly criticized as opportunistic but noted that "our two positions have at least one principle in common—an appeal to the common good. In one context, the union of Church and State is a duty owed by the State to the common good; in another context, equality of cults is a duty owed by the State to the common good."[11]

To this point, Murray clearly embraces the thesis-hypothesis framework common among Catholic theologians of his day. If he had stuck to this line of thought, he would never have encountered the sort of trouble he did with ecclesiastical authorities, and the church's path to the teaching of Vatican II's Declaration on Religious Liberty might have been very different—or might never have been taken at all.

[8] Ibid., 268.
[9] Murray, "Notes on the Theory of Religious Liberty."
[10] Ibid., 16.
[11] Ibid., 17.

There are hints about the direction Murray's thinking would soon take in the importance he placed already on the *historical context* in which the traditional theory had developed. The church's rejection of the theory of religious freedom, he said, stemmed from nineteenth-century Liberalism's "two fundamental principles . . . the absolute autonomy of the individual reason" and "the juridical omnipotence of the state."[12] The state began to treat all religions equally "not out of respect for the consciences of its citizens or concern for their common good, but out of complete indifference to religion and morality as such." This was what Popes Gregory XVI, Pius IX, and Leo had each condemned. Where Liberalism said conscience is God, the church objected that it was our perception of the voice of God and could be mistaken. Where Liberalism understood freedom as absolutely personal sovereignty, the church said it was found in obedience to conscience.

Having taken this first significant step into the conversation about religious freedom, Murray paused. He did not continue the promised series of articles; parts 2 and 3, on the issue's theological and political aspects, never appeared. Decades later, he would speak of being confused during this time and struggling to clarify his thinking. He said he had abandoned the planned articles because he "saw that the logic of his thought would lead, with relatively insignificant differences, to the same conclusions as those of the conservative Catholic view."[13]

Murray wrote little on the topic for about three years, other than a few occasional pieces in *America* that drew attention to current events related to the church-state question (such as a controversy in the Wisconsin legislature over bus transportation of parochial school children, and Protestant protests of President Roosevelt's appointment of the wealthy industrialist Myron Taylor as his personal envoy to Pope Pius XII).[14]

---

[12] Ibid., 279. Note that here the words *Liberalism* and *Liberals* refer to the embrace of modern freedoms such as freedom of conscience, freedom of speech, and freedom of religion. *Liberalism* rejected monarchical government and called for representative democracy.

[13] Thomas T. Love, *John Courtney Murray: Contemporary Church-State Theory* (Garden City, NY: Doubleday, 1965), 40, 48.

[14] John Courtney Murray, "Separation of Church and State," *America* 76 (December 7, 1946): 261–63; "Separation of Church and State: True and False Concepts," *America* 76 (February 15, 1947): 541–45; "The Court Upholds Religious Freedom,"

What emerged three years later, in his next major consideration of the question, would mark a significant development in his thought and would set him out on a journey that would be both dramatic and consequential both for him and for the Catholic Church as a whole.

America 76 (March 8, 1947): 628–30; "Dr. Morrison and the First Amendment," *America* 78 (March 6, 1948): 627–29; "Dr. Morrison and the First Amendment: II," *America* 78 (March 20, 1948): 683–86.

Chapter 5

Considering History
(1948–1949)

At the June 1948 meeting of the Catholic Theological Society of America (CTSA), Murray presented a major paper on the question of whether a "Catholic government" has the duty and the right to repress heretical opinions by law.[1] For the first time, he criticized the reigning "thesis-hypothesis" approach as misleading and no longer useful. He was also critical of the supporting premise that "error has no rights," calling it "meaningless," because "rights are predicated only of persons (or of institutions). If it means anything, it means that error is error; but it is hardly a 'principle' from which to draw any conclusions with regard to the powers of the state."[2]

A New Approach

Murray argued that the key to a better approach to the question lay in a proper understanding of the two distinct roles or ends of the state and the church in modern society. In the Middle Ages, he said, church and state (in Europe) were in fact coextensive and united. The church provided the political as well as spiritual unity of society. A person

---

[1] John Courtney Murray "Governmental Repression of Heresy," in *Proceedings of the Third Annual Convention of the Catholic Theological Society of America* (Bronx: Catholic Theological Society of America, 1948), 26–98. Murray had been slated to deliver the address the previous year but had to bow out because of health problems. Ironically (given events of the years to follow), it was Fr. Joseph Fenton who offered an address in Murray's place that year.

[2] Ibid., 37, 33.

lived as a member of society via membership in the church. In this situation, it was factually true that a threat to the unity of the church also threatened society's well-being and the common good; therefore, by opposing heresy and non-Catholic beliefs, the church was protecting the public order.[3] These historical circumstances were the context in which the thesis-hypothesis theory had begun to form. "Political rulers acted, Popes acted; and then came the theologians—often politically partisan in their sympathies—to think out the theory."[4]

In modern times, however, the situation was vastly different. Church and state were no longer coextensive in fact, and their roles in society were different. Now the state was concerned with "the natural, secular, temporal order of human life." Its purpose was to create or encourage the political, social, economic, and cultural conditions that allow people and society to flourish. By fostering peace, prosperity, justice, and order, the state supports and defends human dignity. This indirectly supports the work of the church, but the state's most direct involvement in that work is to allow the church the freedom to carry out its own work. The church, meanwhile, has a spiritual mission: saving souls. Its purpose is to bring God's grace to humanity by proclaiming its doctrine, administering its sacraments, promoting virtuous daily living, and thereby gathering up all people into the community of salvation willed by God.[5]

Murray granted that in terms of God's law, individuals and groups outside the Catholic Church do not have the right to preach the Gospel and that the church rejects their beliefs. But it is not the role of the state today to enforce this by the coercive power of law on those who choose not to accept it.[6] This was unclear to so many Catholic thinkers because of a failure to distinguish historical circumstances from doctrinal principles (a distinction he would make repeatedly for the next several decades and that would garner much heated opposition). Murray told the CTSA:

> The hypothesis rested, not on the dogma of the Catholic Church as the one true Church, which is unalterable by time, but on a particular concept of the state and of the functions

[3] Ibid., 80, 86–87.
[4] Ibid., 35.
[5] Ibid., 70–76.
[6] Ibid., 83.

of civil government, which was time-conditioned. Today, of course, as in the sixteenth century, and in the thirteenth, and in the fifth, it is unalterably true that heresy ought not to be; it is not endowed by any divine or natural law with the right to exist. But the question is whether a secular government, denominated Catholic, is bound by any divine-positive or natural law unto the duty, and consequently empowered with a right to suppress it. I suggest that the answer is no.[7]

The Opposition: Fenton and Connell

In comments following Murray's presentation, CTSA president Francis Connell suggested that Murray had "not sufficiently considered another doctrine—the Kingship of Jesus Christ." Regardless of social changes, the spiritual and temporal welfare of citizens and society always would pertain to one another. "Hence," he said, "just as the State can prohibit people from preaching the doctrine of free love, so it can prohibit them from preaching, to the detriment of the Catholic citizens, the doctrine that Christ is not present in the Holy Eucharist." Murray's thinking was, Connell concluded, "out of harmony with the traditional belief and attitude of the Church for many centuries. I for one shall continue to hold the traditional view."[8]

Connell's colleague and friend, Joseph Clifford Fenton, also challenged Murray's thinking the following month in an article in the *American Ecclesiastical Review (AER)*, for which he served as editor-in-chief. Fenton and Connell shared an intense interest in defending Catholic teaching against any and all critics. Fenton published article after article in the *AER* insisting on the Catholic faith as the only true religion, the unquestioning acceptance of every papal utterance, and a rigorous understanding of the ancient axiom that "outside the church there is no salvation."[9] Like Connell, Fenton was often combative in approach and

[7] Ibid., 87.

[8] Francis J. Connell, "Discussion of Governmental Repression of Heresy," in *Proceedings of the Third Annual Convention of the Catholic Theological Society of America* (June 28–30, 1948): 98–100.

[9] See, e.g., Joseph Clifford Fenton, "Extra Ecclesiam Nulla Salus," *AER* 110 (April 1944): 300–6; "The Proof of the Church's Divine Origin," *AER* 113 (September

fiercely rejected anything that seemed to threaten distinctive Catholic belief, practice, or culture.[10] He saw the church as living in a perpetual state of siege against the world.[11] He made frequent extended trips to Rome, during which he met almost daily with powerful figures like Cardinal Alfredo Ottaviani, prefect of the Holy Office (later to be called the Congregation for the Doctrine of the Faith), and Cardinal Giuseppe Pizzardo, head of the Congregation for Seminaries and Universities. Indeed, Fenton would eventually be submitting secret reports on Murray and the US church to Ottaviani and vacationing with him on more than one occasion.[12] He frequently refers to Ottaviani in his personal journals as both "the boss" and "Uncle." Ottaviani, as we will see, will figure prominently in Murray's story as it would play out in the years ahead.

The month after Murray's CTSA presentation, Fenton wrote that theological development is "not the substitution of one set of 'contingent' concepts for another, but a restatement in terms understood by men of the present day of those very truths which were expressed and are still expressed in the technical language of scholastic theology." He insisted that a theologian's role is always "to give only a clear, unequivocal, and certain statement of the Church's teaching."[13]

Connell took his own turn at Murray's thinking three months later in the same journal, arguing that Jesus Christ's status as King of the world gives him temporal as well as spiritual power and that all civil rulers "must acknowledge [his] sovereign domination." Such rulers were obliged therefore to participate in an official capacity in Catholic worship, to promote the Catholic religion, and to protect by law Catholic judgments related to marriage and other matters.[14]

1945): 203–19; "The Catholic and the Church," *AER* 113 (November 1945): 376–84; "The Doctrinal Authority of Papal Encyclicals," *AER* 121 (September 1949): 136–50.

[10] See R. Scott Appleby and John Haas, "The Last Supernaturalists: Fenton, Connell, and the Threat of Catholic Indifferentism," *U.S. Catholic Historian* 13, no. 2 (Spring 1995): 23–48.

[11] See, e.g., Joseph Clifford Fenton, "The Church and the State of Siege," *AER* 112 (January 1945): 54–63.

[12] Appleby and Haas, "The Last Supernaturalists," 24n2.

[13] Joseph Clifford Fenton, "New Concepts in Theology," *AER* 119 (July 1948): 56–62, at 61, 60.

[14] Francis J. Connell, "Christ the King of Civil Rulers," *AER* 119 (October 1948): 244–53.

Considering History

In the months that followed, Murray set about further developing his points on the historical context of the question in a series of three articles in *Theological Studies*.[15] These articles carefully explored several crucial historical periods in the ongoing question of the relationship of church and state in history. Though Murray never produced a mono-graph laying out his arguments and vision in an exhaustive way before his death, the matters he addresses in these three articles would surely have formed some of the most important material in such a work.

Because these articles make points about several different historical periods but do not proceed chronologically at all, they can present a challenge to the nonspecialist reader. Rather than consider them in-dividually, I will lay out in five stages what I take to be the historical vision that Murray presents.

A. Gelasius: "Two There Are"

To Murray, the authentic approach of Christian tradition to the re-lationship between church and state was articulated by the fifth-century pope St. Gelasius I. In a famous letter to the Eastern Roman emperor Anastasius I, Gelasius wrote of the duality of powers—the temporal and the spiritual—which governed human society: "Two there are, august Emperor, by which this world is ruled on title of original and sovereign right—the consecrated authority of the priests and the royal power." It is a sentence to which Murray would refer often in the years ahead, sometimes with the three-word shorthand, "Two there are." Murray credited Dominican philosopher-theologian-monk John of Paris (1255–1306) with retrieving the thinking of Gelasius in medieval times.

The temporal ends of society, said Gelasius and John, are peace, justice, and prosperity for the people. A civil ruler has real and distinct power in these areas that comes immediately from God and not by

[15] John Courtney Murray, "St. Robert Bellarmine on the Indirect Power," *Theological Studies* 9 (December 1948): 491–535; "Contemporary Orientations of Catholic Thought on Church and State in the Light of History," *Theological Studies* 10 (June 1949): 177–234; "Current Theology: On Religious Freedom," *Theological Studies* 10 (September 1949): 409–32.

delegation of the pope.[16] But this ruler's powers are limited to these temporal matters. The church's spiritual power, meanwhile, applies to—here he cites the words of John of Paris—"whatever in human affairs is in any way sacred, whatever pertains to the salvation of souls or the worship of God." This "whatever is in any way sacred" marks the boundaries of the church's power, Murray said, and called the idea "the pure essence of Catholic tradition."[17] Within these boundaries falls the preaching of the Gospel, the teaching of doctrine, the administration of the sacraments, and the forming of consciences of believers. Here lies the church's jurisdiction, and the consequences of exercising this power lie in the spiritual order of things.

That doesn't mean there are no temporal consequences to the church's power. By shaping the moral convictions and behavior of those who make up society, the church shapes society itself. By this formation, for example, the people will choose to support or reject what the ruler does. So this spiritual power is by no means less authoritative or effective just because there is no direct temporal power attached to it. It transcends the political order. It is immanent within society, like grace is immanent in nature.[18]

B. The Middle Ages: "One Factual Entity"

"The massive fact of medieval Christendom," Murray wrote, was that the boundaries of the church and the empire were coextensive—the church was society and the empire existed within it. Baptism provided membership in this singular social body, making a person both a Christian and a citizen. "The medieval papacy . . . stood at the center as well as at the summit of this one factual entity that men called christianitas. . . . Civil status and religious status implied one another and were indivisible; one had status within the Church or one had no status."[19]

The power of the medieval temporal ruler was subordinate to that of the pope and came by delegation of the pope. Murray noted that

[16] Murray, "Contemporary Orientations of Catholic Thought on Church and State in the Light of History," 199.

[17] Ibid., 216.

[18] Ibid., 179, 208, 214–15.

[19] Murray, "St. Robert Bellarmine on the Indirect Power," 502, 512.

there was nothing traditional about this. It was a new practice for the time, and the theological theory that justified it simply articulated the practice.[20]

He suggested that the sweeping power of the medieval popes was an important element of the common good at a time when the political order lacked the development necessary to offer a check on the power of a temporal ruler. The medieval king was the government; everything depended on his preferences, whims, and personality. When no one else could, the church could hold him accountable to principles of justice and fairness, even deposing him if he became a tyrant. Society needed this role to be played by the church at the time.[21]

If heresy was opposed by medieval civil rulers, it was not so much because heretics held erroneous religious beliefs but because in this social context, their beliefs were a threat to public order. Heretics were punished not because it was possible but because it was necessary to the common good.[22]

The development of the nation-state with a centralized national monarchy, at the beginning of the fourteenth century, challenged this order of things. This challenge came first in the form of French King Philip IV's (king from 1285 to 1314) demand for the independence of his kingdom and the autonomy of his own rule over against that of the pope. Taking the medieval status quo to be divinely designed, Pope Boniface VIII (who reigned from 1294 to 1303) opposed Philip and strongly asserted this divine design, especially in his famous bull *Unam Sanctam* (1302), insisting that all power, temporal and spiritual, came under the jurisdiction of the pope and that the king was therefore subordinate to the pope. This, Murray suggested, *reflected the contemporary arrangement of things without formally defining it* as Catholic doctrine.[23]

[20] Ibid., 502.

[21] Ibid., 526–32.

[22] Murray, "Current Theology: On Religious Freedom," 431.

[23] Murray, "Contemporary Orientations of Catholic Thought on Church and State in the Light of History," 180.

C. Robert Bellarmine: Transitional Figure

In the early sixteenth century, the theologian-cardinal St. Robert Bellarmine (1542–1621) provided a theological systematization of church-state thinking that Murray calls "an historical achievement of the first order, immensely influential in his own time, and regarded as classic ever since."[24] Living in the immediate aftermath of the Protestant Reformation and in the time of nations that were either officially Catholic or Protestant, Bellarmine opposed those who asserted the divine right of kings, the independence and superiority of a civil ruler's power, and the power of the civil ruler to judge religious matters. He defended the distinction between temporal and spiritual power, the subordination of the temporal to the spiritual, and the strictly spiritual nature of the pope's power.

Because Bellarmine did see the pope as having power in the temporal order when some serious threat to the salvation of souls or the good of the church demanded it, Murray criticized him for sneaking direct temporal power back into the theory after rejecting it. "Bellarmine's indirect power seems to be simply a direct power restricted to exceptional use; but if the Church uses it she must have had it; and in that case the power of the Church is not solely spiritual."[25]

Murray also argued that, despite the importance and influence of Bellarmine's distinction between the two powers, the Italian theologian was prevented by his assumptions from going far enough in his thinking. Although the church and empire as a single social reality had disappeared by Bellarmine's day, Bellarmine theorized as though it had not. Murray noted that Bellarmine expected that situation created by the Reformation to be a passing phenomenon, a temporary factor, and that the restoration of the unity of the church was just a matter of time. He drew conclusions from this that were dependent on these historical circumstances and took his conclusions to be absolute. As a result, Bellarmine defends the papal right to depose a civil ruler and the ruler's duty to exterminate heresy.[26]

[24] Murray, "St. Robert Bellarmine on the Indirect Power," 492.
[25] Ibid., 501.
[26] Ibid., 507–13.

D. The Eighteenth Century: Church vs. Liberalism

The French Revolution of 1789 had jettisoned all deference to tradition, revelation, church, and ecclesial authority. It left in its wake a widespread commitment to the autonomous self and at the same time a theory of state absolutism. It also included widespread rejection and persecution of the Catholic Church.

One aspect of the autonomy promoted by Continental Liberalism was religious freedom, understood as the freedom of every individual to determine for him or herself whether and what to believe, and the duty of the state to sever itself from any support of or interest in religion (and certainly, in the French context, from the Catholic Church). This was the context in which the religious freedom question was addressed in the nineteenth century.

Inheriting the theory of previous centuries, Pope Leo XIII (who reigned as pope from 1878 to 1903) defended the confessional state. Murray insisted Leo's teaching was rooted in historical circumstances and that his conclusions in this regard were not doctrinal in nature.[27]

Within this polemical context, church leaders, in their opposition to all that was dangerous and opposed to church doctrine, missed what was rational, good, and harmonious with the Catholic moral tradition. In a sort of fog of war, in their all-out determination to refute everything about Continental Liberalism, they rejected even what was right about it. Murray wrote that Liberalism "was destructive, of course . . . but it too bore in its depths an intention of nature. . . . It was the fundamental intention, present beneath the welter of false ideology that almost concealed it, to situate the human person at the center of the whole social order."[28]

---

[27] Murray, "Contemporary Orientations of Catholic Thought on Church and State in the Light of History," 184, 232. In an *AER* article soon to follow, Murray would write: "For centuries the problem of Church and State has been the problem of the Church and France. And 'France' here means two things—royal absolutism and the Revolution, both of which, after the French example, became international phenomena. (One would, for instance, more accurately understand certain portions of Leo XIII if one were to substitute the word, 'France,' where he used the term, 'the state.')" See "For the Freedom and Transcendence of the Church," *AER* 126 (January 1952): 28–48, at 44.

[28] Murray, "Contemporary Orientations of Catholic Thought on Church and State in the Light of History," 231.

In particular, Murray said, the church missed the different and even more valid strain of democracy as it developed in the Anglo-Saxon countries—Great Britain and, in particular, the United States. In these nations, democracy didn't mean absolute autonomy of the state or of the self. It was not seen, as it was by Continental Liberalism, as a tool to effect a formal dechristianization of the population.[29]

In the United States, "the first state in the history of the world that was established by the uniquely revolutionary means of a formal constitutional consent," he said, political theory was surely influenced by this eighteenth-century ideology but was not poisoned by it. The essential premise of the First Amendment is not the absolute power of the state (as it is in Continental Liberalism) but the distinction of jurisdictions of state and church, the dualism that governs the life of society, which was defended by Gelasius in the fifth century, John of Paris in the fourteenth, and Bellarmine in the seventeenth.[30]

E. Twentieth Century: "The Civil Order Grew Up"

The twentieth century, Murray argued, presented an entirely new context in which to approach the question of religious freedom. Central to this context is the rise of democracy, which Murray calls "a political development of the first magnitude, the greatest since the rise of the nation-state, and greater than it."[31]

---

[29] Ibid., 186–87.

[30] Ibid., 187. Elsewhere, Murray would write, "The great question, raised for the first time in the nineteenth century, [was], 'Who are the people?' Actually, the first great historic answer to the question was given in the United States; but the din raised by the conflict with Continental Liberalism was too great to permit the voice of America (ironically, a deist and Protestant voice giving a Catholic answer) to be heard in European canon-law classrooms. In fact, to this day European authors of textbooks *de iure publico* seem unaware that there is any difference between Jacobin democracy and Anglo-Saxon democracy, or between 'the sovereignty of the people' in the sense of the men of '89 and 'government of the people, for the people, and by the people' in the sense of Lincoln." See "The Problem of 'The Religion of the State,'" *AER* 124 (May 1951): 327–52, at 336n10.

[31] Murray, "Contemporary Orientations of Catholic Thought on Church and State in the Light of History," 181.

While in medieval times the church was moral judge of a ruler's justice and fairness, now the people are. The governing agency is no longer empire or king; citizens, through democratic institutions, govern themselves.[32] Murray offered the image of an adolescent dependent on the authority and guidance of his parents. But adolescents grow up and rightly differentiate themselves from that authority and no longer need it. Once grown up, they may make some poor choices, but still the differentiation is necessary and right. "So it was with the civil order. It grew up; it became a State; and as a State it differentiated itself from the Church, as a society in its own right, with its own institutions to direct and correct its action."[33]

The key idea to democracy is that the people share in power and hold leaders accountable. This sharing in power depends on the democratic institutions known as civil liberties—freedom of opinion, association, speech, press, and religious expression. These civil liberties form an organic whole, a system of liberty that is part of the common good. Because they are an organic whole, a government cannot pick and choose which liberties to grant.[34]

Freedom of religion as it is expressed in the first amendment of the US Constitution, Murray said, recognizes the primacy of the spiritual inasmuch as it is based on the idea that the spiritual life, the conscience, of each person and the values that grow from it are supreme over the values of the state. While it forbids establishment of a church by the state, it also provides, via religious liberty, for "the immunity of conscience from governmental coercion, and the freedom of conscience to impose on the government the moral demands that are the permanent exigencies of the human spirit in consequence of its obligation 'to obey God rather than man.'"[35]

Civil liberties, including freedom of religion, are therefore what now ensure the primacy of the spiritual end of man over the temporal and the lay state. "The Church," wrote Murray, "is free to form the consciences

---

[32] Ibid., 193.

[33] Murray, "St. Robert Bellarmine on the Indirect Power," 530.

[34] Murray, "Contemporary Orientations of Catholic Thought on Church and State in the Light of History," 181–82.

[35] Ibid., 188–89.

of her members; and they as citizens are free to conform the life of the City to the demands of their consciences." Civil rights are now politically necessary to the freedom of the church. They are the safeguards of that freedom, which is the central doctrinal principle that was in play all along. American political theory therefore provides "a political category in which the contemporary problem of religious freedom can receive its valid theoretical statement."[36]

Murray concludes colorfully:

> In 800 A.D., Leo III had a right to crown Charlemagne as Emperor of the Romans; but this was because it was 800 A.D. If there were a Christendom tomorrow—a Christian world-government in a society whose every member was baptized— the Pope, for all the fullness of his apostolic authority, would not have the slightest shadow of a right to "crown" so much as a third-class postmaster.[37]

[36] Ibid., 224–25, 234, 190.
[37] Murray, "St. Robert Bellarmine on the Indirect Power," 534–35.

Chapter 6

The Battle Is Engaged
(1950–1952)

I t did not take long for other theologians to engage the ideas that Murray carefully laid out in his *Theological Studies* articles. A response came in the pages of the *American Ecclesiastical Review*, and a remarkable theological conversation ensued.

Scholarly Debate, Personal Snarls

The first rejoinder to Murray's work came in an article from seminary professor Msgr. George W. Shea.[1] Identifying Murray as the primary opponent of the permanent and unalterable thesis-hypothesis approach in Catholic doctrine, Shea denied that he had made a compelling case. Citing a list of standard late nineteenth- and early twentieth-century theological manuals, he insisted that each person individually and society as a whole had a moral duty to worship God. The *state* owed God worship, which meant in practice that people in positions of civil authority must participate in worship in an official capacity. Since Catholicism is the only true religion, the state had "the duty of accepting Catholicism, its creed, code, cult" (that is, its faith, its moral law, and its worship). This necessarily entailed the establishment of Catholicism as the religion of the state. "How else could the state, qua state, in truth accept and profess Catholicism, together with the tenet that it alone is the true religion?"[2]

---

[1] George W. Shea, "Catholic Doctrine and 'The Religion of the State,'" *AER* 123 (September 1950): 161–74.
[2] Ibid., 167, 168.

Acknowledging that some of Pope Leo's reasons for endorsing the idea of the religion of the state might well have been, as Murray suggested, historically contingent, Shea insisted that not all of them were. Specifically, there was at least one doctrinal reason: the state must worship God "because it is a creature of God." He went on to cite passages from Leo XIII and Pius X that insist on the duty of the state to worship God.[3]

Finally, Shea argued the concept of a state religion included the right and duty for the state to suppress heresy. To support the assertion, Shea cited a passage of canon law that said local bishops have the right to approve or disapprove religion teachers and textbooks in public schools. Since this in effect gave bishops the right to suppress heresy in public schools, Shea said, then the church must have that right.[4]

Fenton provided Murray with the forum to respond to Shea in the May 1951 issue of *AER*, marking Murray's first appearance in the journal. In a brief editor's note, printed as a footnote attached to the title of the article, Fenton commented, "The Editor . . . believes that it is only fair to add that he does not share Fr. Murray's views on the subject of this article."[5] (Clearly bothered by this, Murray would include with his next submission to the *AER* a letter to Fenton asking that he either print it without editorial comment or not print it at all. In a response, Fenton accepted the article—which would be printed in January 1952—but scolded Murray for his "lofty lecture" on editorial practice. Murray responded by trying to justify his request and asked, "Please let us not get into some sort of personal snarl. . . . There is no need of our quarreling, is there?"[6])

Murray acknowledged that Pope Leo XIII's writing seemed to support the idea that Catholicism ought be recognized as the state church in all cases. But he argued that Leo was in fact not formally teaching that the state ought by nature to be Catholic, to the active exclusion of other religions; rather, Leo was rejecting "the French Revolutionary

[3] Ibid., 170.

[4] Ibid., 173–74.

[5] John Courtney Murray, "The Problem of 'The Religion of the State,'" *AER* 124 (May 1951): 327–52, at 327.

[6] Rev. John Courtney Murray Papers, Box 1, Folder 70, Georgetown University Library, Special Collections Research Center, Washington, DC.

thesis that the state ought by nature to be atheist." Leo's rejection of the Revolution's attack on "juridical and social dualism, under the primacy of the spiritual" had come to be understood as dogmatic endorsement of Catholicism as religion of the state, a jump that ought not to have been made.[7]

The truly traditional and authentic Catholic doctrine that Leo was defending, and that must always be defended, Murray wrote, is the *libertas Ecclesiae*, the freedom of the church to guide its life, teach its doctrine, and conduct its worship unencumbered by the state. This is the central principle (and Leo's "key concept") that must be emphasized in understanding the problem.[8]

Murray questioned Shea's assertion that the state is "a creature of God," a phrase that is not used to describe the state in Pope Leo's writings or any other magisterial documents. The state, he says, is a set of institutions created by people to organize social control and services. (Murray asks if Shea would say we must speak of the American presidency, Congress, and Supreme Court as creatures of God.) The state is not a person and cannot, therefore, make an act of faith.[9]

"In the Event That Fr. Murray's Teaching Is True"

The following month, Fenton offered a roundup article, summarizing the Shea-Murray discussion thus far, making brief mention of Shea's article and spending the bulk of his space criticizing Murray. "In the event that Fr. Murray's teaching is true," he wrote,

> then it would seem that our students of sacred theology and of public ecclesiastical law have been sadly deceived for the past few centuries. They have been told that the state has an obligation to worship God according to the precepts and the rites of the true religion. . . . It is hard to believe that any Catholic could be convinced that an entire section of Catholic teaching about the Church itself could be so imperfect.[10]

[7] Murray, "The Problem of 'The Religion of the State,'" 334, 340, 352.
[8] Ibid., 328n3.
[9] Ibid., 330n6, 344n14.
[10] Joseph Clifford Fenton, "The Status of the Controversy," *AER* 124 (June 1951): 451–58, at 452, 456.

Fenton emphasized the distinction between a state's objective duty to worship God (which exists in all cases) and its subjective duty (which exists only in cases of states where "the existence of the objective obligation is realized," or as was more commonly put at the time, in a Catholic society).[11]

Connell followed with a significant article in the following issue of the *AER*. Criticizing Murray's "very definite and radical departure from what has hitherto been commonly regarded as Catholic doctrine,"[12] he emphasized again the authority of Christ as "King and Lord of the world" whose authority extends even to civil rulers and their governments. He offered specific examples in which Christ's dominion trumped natural law and the natural right of rulers to govern, including the right of missionaries to preach the Gospel in any land, regardless of local civil law; the obligation of a government to accept the church's policies about marriage, even where civil laws differ; and the canon law forbidding civil officials, under pain of excommunication, to arrest or put on trial Catholic bishops and cardinals ("in order that the dignity and liberty of [Christ's] earthly representatives might be more effectively maintained").[13]

Connell acknowledged that the role of the state is to promote the temporal well-being of its citizens but insisted that a person "cannot have true *temporal* happiness (that is, happiness in the present life) unless he enjoys *supernatural* blessings; and consequently, if the state is concerned with the temporal welfare of its citizens, it will have some concern for their supernatural happiness in the world."[14] And so it has an obligation to investigate the church's claims of divine origin, officially accept Catholicism, and restrict propaganda and proselytizing by any other religions or denominations.

The January 1952 *AER* included a lengthy response from Murray, along with a "Reply to Father Murray" by Connell immediately following it. Murray's sharply worded article accused Connell of having "no understanding of the content of my position" and "no understanding

---

[11] Ibid., 452.

[12] Francis J. Connell, "The Theory of the 'Lay State,'" *AER* 125 (July 1951): 7–18, at 17–18.

[13] Ibid., 12–16.

[14] Ibid., 17.

of the historical significance of John of Paris." He noted a "lack of breadth, depth, comprehension, and clarity" and a "confusion" in Connell's work.[15]

Murray wrote that Connell gave the state more power than it ought to have by suggesting a government should "permit" missionaries to preach the Gospel, since missionaries don't need a government's permission to do that, and by suggesting that a state has an obligation to reach a judgment about the Catholic Church's claims to divine origins, since no civil ruler has the power to pass judgment on the church.[16]

Murray also accused Connell of a faulty "conceptualism" by speaking of the state as a sort of person when he suggests it must investigate the claims of Catholicism. "Upon whom does [this obligation] rest—the Federal government, or the State government, or county, municipal and township governments—or upon all (or perhaps only some) of the hundreds of thousands of men in this country who hold political office and therefore may qualify as 'civil rulers'?" The state, Murray said, cannot make an act of faith. Connell's conception of what a state ought to do with regard to Catholicism was only realistic in the context of an absolute monarchy; as a result, he said, Connell effectively denied the church's transcendence to all political forms.[17]

Finally, Murray emphasized Connell's failure to recognize that the church's approach to church-state issues were too dependent on the historical circumstance of the conflict between church and state that resulted from the French Revolution.

In his reply, Connell insisted in his first sentence that "Fr. Murray has chosen to attack me instead of clarifying and defending his own views." Murray's comments, Connell said, amounted to "a somewhat complicated way of saying that I am rather stupid."[18] He said Murray's criticism about giving the state more authority over the church than it had was valid only if a particular meaning of the word *permit* was imposed on his comments, but he noted there was another equally

[15] John Courtney Murray, "For the Freedom and Transcendence of the Church," *AER* 126 (January 1952): 28–48, at 28n1, 32, 42.

[16] Ibid., 29–32.

[17] Ibid., 33–38, quote at 34.

[18] Francis J. Connell, "Reply to Father Murray," *AER* 126 (January 1952): 49–59, at 49, 58.

valid way of understanding the word. Contra Murray's claims about Connell's conceptualism, Connell noted that while a state cannot make an act of faith, civil officials can and ought to investigate the reasons that make the Church's claims credible and therefore conclude that the church should exercise its ministry unimpeded, while the same sort of freedom clearly ought not to be granted to any and all religious claims.[19]

Later that year, Fenton offered his most comprehensive statement to date, outlining the basic theological principles involved in the entire question. It was a classic restatement of the thesis-hypothesis theory, which, he wrote, derives from the fact that every human being "and every social unit" owes God the debt of worship and that the only objectively acceptable form of that worship is Catholic worship.[20]

During this same period, Murray's thinking also received critical attention in the pages of *La Civiltà Cattolica,* an Italian journal considered (then and now) to be a "semiofficial" publication of the Vatican because its contents receive the approval of the Vatican secretariat of state before publication. Between April 1950 and September 1952, the journal published nineteen articles on the topic of church-state relations and religious freedom, all of them defending the classic thesis-hypothesis theory and critical of theologians who questioned it. Though Murray was not mentioned in any of them by name, three of these essays in particular were, as theologian Joseph Komonchak observes, "unmistakably directed against Murray's views."[21]

Behind the Scenes

During this same time period, the conflict over Murray's take on Catholic doctrine on church-state relations began to reach considerably beyond the pages of theological journals. Some significant developments in the story were happening outside the public eye as well.

---

[19] Ibid., 50–52, 53–54.

[20] Joseph Clifford Fenton, "Principles Underlying Traditional Church-State Doctrine," *AER* 126 (June 1952): 452–62.

[21] Joseph A. Komonchak, "The Silencing of John Courtney Murray," in *Cristianesimo nella Storia: Saggi in Onore di Giuseppe Alberigo,* ed. A. Melloni, et al. (Bologna: Il Mulino, 1996), 657–702, at 666.

On August 1, 1950, Francis Connell sent a letter about Murray to Cardinal Pizzardo, prefect of the Congregation for Seminaries and Universities. He enclosed the text of Murray's 1948 CTSA address and also a recently published article of his own. He insisted that Murray's work was contrary to the teaching of Popes Leo XIII and Pius XII and pointed out that Murray was getting positive coverage in the American press.[22]

This was, in fact, the first of many letters about Murray that Connell would send to Vatican officials over the following twelve years, frequently including the suggestion that Murray's views demanded public repudiation by the church. In a February 1952 response to one letter that had been directed to Archbishop Amleto Cicognani, the Vatican's apostolic delegate to the United States, the archbishop assured Connell that he had forwarded "certain materials on this question" to the Holy See. "I am sure that it will be seriously considered," he wrote, "but we know that the investigation and study take time."[23]

Murray, too, was active behind the scenes. In late September 1950, at an international Catholic conference on ecumenism in Grottaferrata, Italy,[24] he met Msgr. Giovanni Battista Montini, a longtime official of the Vatican Secretariat of State. Since 1944, Montini had been, with one other official, running that office directly under Pope Pius XII, in the absence of an officially appointed secretary of state, so he was certainly a powerful Vatican official who had the ear of the pope. (At the time Murray met him, Montini was still four years from being named archbishop of Milan and thirteen years from his election as pope, when he would take the name Paul VI.) By Murray's account, he discussed

[22] Ibid., 660.

[23] Ibid.; see also Joseph A. Komonchak, "'The Crisis in Church-State Relationships in the U.S.A.' A Recently Discovered Text by John Courtney Murray," *The Review of Politics* 61, no. 4 (Autumn 1999): 675–714, at 678.

[24] Another participant in this conference was the Dominican theologian Yves Congar (who would, more than a decade later, work closely with Murray at Vatican II, where both would serve as theological experts). In his personal journal, Congar described the paper Murray delivered at this 1950 conference as "quite remarkable" for its "precision, quality, and intellectual rigor." Cited in Komonchak, "The Crisis in Church-State Relationships in the U.S.A.," 680.

the topic of church-state relations with Montini "in some detail" and was encouraged by their conversation.[25]

In late October, Murray prepared and mailed a long memo for Montini titled "The Crisis in Church-State Relationships in the U.S.A."[26] In the memo, Murray noted that American society was marked by a new secularism, a firm belief in democracy as the best hope for stability and freedom, and a deep distrust of the Catholic Church because of its current stance on religious freedom. He argued at some length that "the Church's traditional doctrine can be vitally adapted to the legitimate political exigencies of a democratically organized state," noting the key American and Catholic principles in question. He called for formal clarification of the idea of the state, society, and democracy in Catholic teaching and a correction of the false impression that the church envisions a sort of Catholic police state as the ideal form of government. Such developments would yield "a Church-State doctrine that will not be an obstacle, but a help, in the Church's apostolate in the contemporary world."[27]

In May 1951, Montini passed the document along to others, soliciting their opinion of its contents. These included Cardinal Samuel Stritch (the archbishop of Chicago) and Connell. It was also provided to the Holy Office.[28] Connell responded to Montini's request almost immediately. (It is not clear that Montini revealed to Connell who had written it, but Connell was surely familiar enough with Murray's writings to realize it.) He wrote that it was hard to see how ideas in the memo "can be harmonized with revealed truth." The church's teaching can never change, he insisted, and so Catholics should get

---

[25] The quotation is from a 1953 letter written by Murray to Fr. Robert Leiber, cited in Komonchak, "The Silencing of John Courtney Murray," 661n10.

[26] Murray also sent a copy of the memo to his friend Clare Booth Luce as a resource in her preparations for her February 1953 confirmation hearings before the US Senate for her appointment as US Ambassador to the Vatican (Komonchak, "The Crisis in Church-State Relationships in the U.S.A.," 681).

[27] Komonchak, "The Crisis in Church-State Relationships in the U.S.A.," quotations at 694, 704. This Komonchak article includes the complete text (seventeen pages) of Murray's memo to Montini, as well as the full texts of the commentaries by Stritch and Connell noted below.

[28] Ibid., 682–83.

used to being hated for it and priests publishing ideas such as those in the memo "should be admonished to be silent, at least until the Holy See has given a decision."[29]

Stritch did not initially reply to Montini, but Montini asked again in May 1952. Stritch finally responded by writing that he thought it seemed clear that Pope Leo's teaching on church-state relations was doctrinal in nature and not simply a reflection of contemporary opinion, and he restated the thesis-hypothesis theory.[30]

Montini's sharing of this memo would prove to be an important factor as Murray's story played out in the years ahead.

Blanshard's Book

We should note, before closing this chapter, an important part of the context in which this theological sparring in *AER* was happening. In May 1949, Beacon Press published Paul Blanshard's *American Freedom and Catholic Power* (which had its origins as a series of articles that had appeared in the journal *The Nation* the previous year). In the book, Blanshard took broad aim at "the Catholic problem," raising a cry of alarm against "the place of Catholic power in our national life."[31] He boldly criticized a wide range of Catholic beliefs and practices, which he presented in a harsh, unnuanced, and sometimes distorted way. Opposition to birth control was "the most important part of [the church's] sexual code," he said; the church opposed the study of science and history and promoted instead superstitious beliefs; Catholic schools were divisive elements in American society, and most white criminals were Catholic. (Reflecting one strong current of thought at the time, Blanshard also lambasted the church for its opposition to eugenic sterilization "designed to protect society against the production of feebleminded citizens.")[32] Blanshard drew the book to its conclusion with a long chapter on "the Catholic Plan for America," offering a series

[29] Ibid., 711, 713.

[30] Ibid., 706–7.

[31] Paul Blanshard, *American Freedom and Catholic Power* (Boston: Beacon Press, 1949), 3.

[32] Ibid., 151.

of amendments to the Constitution that Americans could count on if the church got its way, making the United States "a Catholic Republic," outlawing public education, and repealing the First Amendment.[33] Of course, the Catholic thesis-hypothesis theory of religious freedom fed into Blanshard's vision quite easily, and he made ample use of it.

Nativist, anti-Catholic sentiments had been latent in the American cultural landscape for over a century, and Blanshard keyed into them quite effectively. The book sold forty thousand copies in its first three months, making it, in the words of one historian, "the most unusual best-seller of 1949 and 1950."[34] Its success made religious freedom, and criticism of the Catholic Church over the issue, a topic of chic conversation for some time, a state of things that carried on in many ways throughout the decade. (One popular 1960 book, *American Culture and Catholic Schools*, written by an ex-Catholic ex-priest, for example, took up Blanshard's style in a three hundred–page screed against the Catholic school system, which the author said was designed for brainwashing and the production of "shock troops" for the church.[35])

In addressing the topic of religious freedom, therefore, Murray and Fenton were stepping into what was already a heated discussion in the broader American culture.

[33] Ibid., 266–69.

[34] John T. McGreevy, *Catholicism and American Freedom: A History* (New York: W. W. Norton, 2003), 66–168.

[35] Emmett McLoughlin, *American Culture and Catholic Schools* (New York: Lyle Stuart, 1960).

Chapter 7

Digging Deeper: The Leo Articles
(1952–1954)

The debate that took place on the pages of the *American Ecclesiastical Review* between 1950 and 1952 prompted Murray to explore more carefully the ground on which his critics stood and to refine his arguments. The result was his construction of a crucial part of his theological project: a series of articles that Joseph Komonchak has called his greatest scholarly contribution and that Michael Schuck has called "the most impressive pieces of Catholic political theology ever written by a North American theologian."[1]

Beginning in the December 1952 issue of *Theological Studies* and continuing in those of March 1953, June 1953, December 1953, and March 1954, he published a series of articles that offered an assiduous presentation and interpretation of the teaching of Pope Leo XIII (pope from 1878 to 1903) on church-state relations in general and religious freedom in particular.[2] Murray also wrote a sixth article, intended to

---

[1] Joseph Komonchak, "John Courtney Murray," in *The Encyclopedia of American Catholic History*, ed. Michael Glazier and Thomas J. Shelley (Collegeville, MN: Liturgical Press, 1997), 996; Michael J. Schuck, "John Courtney Murray's American Stories," in *Finding God in All Things: Celebrating Bernard Lonergan, John Courtney Murray, and Karl Rahner* (New York: Fordham University Press, 2007), 83–91, at 86.

[2] In order of publication, those articles by Murray are: "The Church and Totalitarian Democracy," *Theological Studies* 13 (December 1952): 525–63; "Leo XIII on Church and State: The General Structure of the Controversy," *Theological Studies* 14 (March 1953): 1–30; "Leo XIII: Separation of Church and State," *Theological Studies* 14 (June 1953): 145–214; "Leo XIII: Two Concepts of Government," *Theological*

be the conclusion of the series, but due to the objections of Roman censors, it never appeared in the journal.[3]

To Murray, what Leo had taught, and what it meant, was a crucial aspect of the problem for two reasons: Leo had emphasized the "Gelasian dualism" that was so important to Murray's conception of the issue, but he had also been an active opponent (like Ottaviani and Fenton) of the separation of church and state and of religious freedom. He could not approach the topic of religious freedom—at least not in a way that would provide a response to accusations that his approach was unfaithful to past papal teaching—without giving due attention to Leo's magisterium, and so due attention he gave it.

Murray's "Leo articles" are long—taken together, they cover about 260 pages in print—and densely argued. J. Leon Hooper's description of them as "a long, twisting series"[4] is pretty accurate. They are sometimes repetitious and often difficult reading. But they represent the core of Murray's thinking on this topic. It is unfortunate that Murray himself did not live long enough to publish them together in book form and strange that to this day they exist nowhere together in published form. Because Murray tends to move, over the course of the six articles, a bit unevenly, forward and back, in his argument, I have chosen to synthesize in the pages below the overall course of his thinking rather than address each article sequentially.

Murray was adamant that understanding Pope Leo's political/cultural context is essential to properly understanding his teaching on religious freedom and its lasting significance. Murray repeatedly pointed to two aspects of this context as particularly crucial. Both grew from the Enlightenment, took sharp expression in the French Revolution, and continued their ascendancy in Leo's late nineteenth-century Europe. These are *the rise of a "state absolutism"* and *a philosophy of unlimited freedom and the absolute autonomy of individual reason.*

Studies 14 (December 1954): 551–67; and "Leo XIII: Two Concepts of Government II: Government and the Order of Culture," *Theological Studies* 15 (March 1954): 1–33.

[3] It was published forty years later, as "Leo XIII and Pius XII: Government and the Order of Religion" in John Courtney Murray, *Religious Liberty: Catholic Struggles with Pluralism*, ed. J. Leon Hooper (Louisville, KY: Westminster/John Knox, 1993), 49–125.

[4] J. Leon Hooper, "Murray and Day: A Common Enemy, A Common Cause?," *U.S. Catholic Historian* 24, no. 1 (Winter 2006): 45–61, at 50.

State Absolutism

The theory of government that dominated Europe in Leo's day was, Murray said, one in which government held authority over all aspects of social existence, and there was no place for the church in that existence. "The final sovereignty even in 'mixed matters' which concerned both Church and State indisputably fell to the State," Murray wrote.[5] According to this "state absolutism" (or "totalitarian democracy"), the only important aspect of human life was the political; the only important truths were political; and social morality must be homogenous, both determined and enforced by the state. If the church had any place at all, it was purely a private and personal one.

In Leo's time, that specifically meant laws (recently enacted in France) that involved the dissolving of the Jesuits and other teaching orders, the establishment of schools to train secular teachers, the suppression of degrees from Catholic universities, the abolition of allowing nuns to teach high school, and the reduction of the number of army chaplains.[6] "The power now stood in the service of a militant secular faith."[7] The adamantly secularist philosophy on which these laws were based was the "ideological enemy" that Leo faced, and his teaching must be understood in that context. He was completely preoccupied by this reality, and "this preoccupation and purpose impart to all of Leo XIII's utterances on the Church-State problem a powerful polemical bias."[8]

To Leo and to most people in Europe, *this is what separation of church and state was about: separating the church from all aspects of social life.* Society was nearly an entirely subordinate category to the state. Murray said the idea had been expressed well by King Louis XIV's statement that "The state is me," except that leaders of the French Revolution had changed the first person singular to a plural: "The state is us."[9]

Against this enemy, Leo insisted that there is a "dualism" in society's structure that must be recognized and respected: there are two

---

[5] Murray, "The Church and Totalitarian Democracy," 526.

[6] Ibid., 549.

[7] Murray, "Leo XIII: Separation of Church and State," 156.

[8] Murray, "Leo XIII on Church and State," 13.

[9] Ibid., 21; cf. Murray, "Leo XIII and Pius XII," 49–125, at 52.

elements to human existence and human society, the civil and the spiritual, and so there are properly two "powers" to guide them. The civil realm and the spiritual realm each have their own powers or authorities—government and the church—which ought not to interfere with each other but ought to exist in harmony. Murray calls this "the Gelasian thesis," after Pope Gelasius's well-known "Two there are" principle mentioned in chapter 5 above.

To Leo, the purpose of civil government is to order society, to create the social conditions under which society and those living in it may flourish. The church must allow government the space to do this work. The purpose of the church is to attend to "whatever is in any way sacred in human affairs, whatever has relation to the salvation of souls or to the worship of God, whether it be such by its own nature or regarded as such by reason of the purpose to which it is referred."[10] The "sacred" things in human affairs include, as Murray explained Leo's thought,

> the husband-wife relationship, the parent-child relationship (including education), the political obligation, the human dignity of the worker, the equality of men as all equally in the image of God, the moral values inherent in economic life, the works of charity and justice which are the native expression of the human and Christian spirit, the patrimony of ideas which are the foundation of human society—the ideas of law, freedom, justice, property, moral obligation, civic obedience, legitimate rule, etc., etc. There is also the thing, sacred in its destination, whereby the Church occupies ground in this world, namely, her legitimate property. But the chiefly sacred thing in the temporal order, in Leo's eyes, is the inner unity, integrity, and peace of man, who is both Christian and citizen.[11]

Just as the church must allow government the space to do the work proper to it, so government must give the church the freedom to carry out its own role. The theme of "the freedom of the church" plays a major part in Leo's thinking, as Murray makes clear.[12]

---

[10] Murray, "Leo XIII: Separation of Church and State," 207.

[11] Ibid., 209.

[12] Murray provides a selection of Leo's major Gelasian texts in ibid., 192ff.

Absolute Autonomy of Reason

The second aspect of Leo's context that Murray saw as crucial was the Enlightenment idea, which had taken root in culture and politics, that humanity is utterly free by nature and that the judgment of an individual's conscience is subject to no law. This "'outlaw individual conscience' . . . would pretend to make its own subjective judgments the ultimate arbiter of truth and error, of right and wrong."[13]

It was a philosophy of extreme individualism and subjectivism, utterly opposed to the (Catholic) idea that there is a moral law to which all are subject and which can and should be expressed in positive (human) laws.[14] Indeed, the teaching of the church and the practice of the Catholic religion came to be seen, by the proponents of this thinking, as a principle enemy to be defeated. "There is unlimited freedom for everybody's ideas and everybody's action—except for Catholic ideas and for the action of the Church."[15]

In continental Europe, religious freedom and the other modern liberties (freedom of speech and the press, for example) were the expression of this philosophy. They were not understood simply as the right to freedom from interference from outside forces on these personal concerns; *they were understood as the rejection of God, faith, institutionalized religion, and the role of these realities in the public sphere.* And so in rejecting the modern liberties like freedom of speech and freedom of religion, Leo was rejecting their philosophical premises and their place within a particular political theory.[16] Murray wrote:

> Leo XIII could not but have constantly in mind the fact that these institutions were not advocated in the new polity as genuine expressions of the principle and method of freedom, but as engines of war upon the Catholic Church. They were concretely part of the whole dynamism of a Jacobin movement. As such, they were "of the enemy," and hence as damnable as he.[17]

---

[13] Murray, "Leo XIII: Two Concepts of Government II," 2.
[14] Murray, "Leo XIII on Church and State," 18; Murray, "Leo XIII and Pius XII," 51.
[15] Murray, "Leo XIII on Church and State," 27.
[16] Murray, "Leo XIII: Two Concepts of Government II," 2.
[17] Murray, "The Church and Totalitarian Democracy," 562.

Also important to Murray in understanding Leo's rejection of religious freedom is Leo's conception of government and the people governed. Government, for Leo, had a paternal role, because the people it governed were rather ignorant masses, easily led to accept any ideas proposed them because they were unable to critically consider them. And there were fanatical people who wished to exploit that ignorance in order to impose their atheist ideas. "A form of intellectual and spiritual aggression was afoot, directed against the Catholic masses, who were helpless to defend themselves because they were ignorant," Murray explained.[18] He wrote:

> Leo XIII considered that the illiterate Catholic masses were in effect children. Their ignorance made them incapable of self-direction. Worse still, they were being directed—indeed manipulated—from above, by evil men, in a direction which would lead to social ruin. These quasi-children were therefore in danger, and the danger to them was a danger likewise to society. Moreover, they were helpless, "absolutely unable, or able only with the greatest difficulty" to protect themselves.[19]

For that reason, the government cannot be neutral about which moral ideas are proposed for acceptance to the people. To Leo, Murray said, "Government must take a side. Concretely, it must positively favor and protect the human heritage against those who would dissipate it by the corrosion of doubt, denial, or cynicism."[20]

The Anglo-American Principles of Government

Unfortunately, Murray argued, Pope Leo was unfamiliar with the principles of the quite different Anglo-American legal/political tradition, expressed in a constitutional and limited government of, by, and for the people. He did not realize that the separation of church and state and the modern freedoms he rejected could take a different form because the philosophical foundations on which they were grounded

---

[18] Ibid., 17.
[19] Ibid., 19. The internal quote is from Leo's encyclical *Libertas*.
[20] Ibid., 12.

in Europe might elsewhere be rooted in a very different, and far more acceptable, philosophy. "The Roman advisers of Leo XIII knew their Rousseau," Murray wrote; "they had probably never heard of the *Federalist* papers."[21]

In the Anglo-American tradition, society and the state are not co-terminous; society is not inferior to the state or subsumed into the state. The state, rather, is one (albeit important) part of society,[22] "a legal association for limited purposes."[23] This difference, Murray said, is "decisive."[24] Several key passages from Murray's June 1953 article offer a helpful taste of Murray's thinking on this.

> The American concept of separation of Church and state . . . is a consequence of the distinction between society and state. It is a consequence of the fact that society, the people, has made to government only a limited grant of powers. It is a consequence of the general theory of a pluralism of powers whereby society is directed. Undoubtedly the distinction between Church and state is exaggerated. But it is one thing to exaggerate a distinction into a separation, as in the American case; it is quite another thing to obliterate the distinction in a false unification, as in the Continental case. In the American case the essential lines of the medieval structure of politics are still somehow visible; in the Continental case they are destroyed utterly.[25]

> The First Amendment has no religious overtones whatever; that is, it does not imply any ultimate vision of the nature of man and society. It does not veil any pretense on the part of the state, to embody ultimate values. . . . Its purpose is not to separate religion from society, but only from the order of law. It implies no denial of God over both society and state, no negation of the social necessity and value of religion, no assertion that the affairs of society and state are to be conducted in disregard of the natural or divine law, or even of ecclesiastical

---

[21] Ibid., 551.
[22] Murray, "Leo XIII: Separation of Church and State," 151–52.
[23] Murray, "Leo XIII on Church and State," 21.
[24] Murray, "Leo XIII: Separation of Church and State," 152.
[25] Ibid.

laws. It is not a political transcription of the religion of laicism. It is a legal rule, not a piece of secular ecclesiology.[26]

Hence the manner in which the Catholic Church exists in American society is not the same as the manner of existence possessed by the Church under the Continental *ius commune*. In the latter case, the Church was legally free to be only what the sovereign society-state legally and authoritatively declared her to be, namely, a voluntary association owing its corporative existence to civil law. In the American case, the Church is completely free to be whatever she is. The law does not presume to make any declarations about her nature, nor does she owe her existence within society to any legal statute. In a word, the Continental *ius commune* denied to the Church the right to declare her own nature; the First Amendment denies to the state the right to declare the nature of the Church.[27]

Moreover, it is not a "happy inconsistency" when the American legislator is inspired by Christian principles. Such an inspiration is entirely consistent with the American concept of the state and society; it is by no means outlawed, as in the Continental concept, by the American legal rule of separation of Church and state. This is not to say that Federal and State legislation in the United States is always obedient to such inspiration. The point is that the American legislator is under no necessity to cast himself in the role of a Continental anti-clerical. American legislation does not on principle repudiate the demands of Christian morality, because, unlike the Continental "separate" society-state, it does not pretend to have an ethical and quasi-religious substance of its own.[28]

It should be already clear that American separation may enter a valid plea of "not guilty" on the two basic counts in the papal indictment of Continental separation. The first count in the indictment bore upon the social and juridical monism that was the immediate premise of Continental separation. . . . Ameri-

---

[26] Ibid., 152–53.
[27] Ibid., 168.
[28] Ibid., 174–75.

can separation is not based on any such monist theory. . . .
The second count in the papal indictment bore upon the social
apostasy inherent in Continental separation. This apostasy
consisted in the conscious repudiation of the Christian and rational truths. . . . However, American separation has no such
pseudo-religious meaning or consequences. It does not entail
the exile of God or of the Church from American society.[29]

The American political tradition was, to Murray, not only not opposed to Catholic principles; it was, in fact, a strong expression of
them. Where the Continental separation of church and state was a
result of the complete corruption of the medieval heritage of political
philosophy, the American version flowed far more faithfully, though
"in secularized and Protestantized form," from it.[30] Having avoided the
state absolutism that ruined Continental politics, American political
tradition had "remained substantially true to the great tradition."[31]

Murray wrote, "Only the superficial interpreter or the man of ill
will—only those who are by definition not scholars—can maintain
that Leo XIII was against democracy, as this term is understood in the
Anglo-American tradition. On the contrary, he combated a conspiracy
against the moral principles upon which Anglo-American democracy
rests."[32]

Timeless Teaching, Contingent Opinions

Considering all of this, Murray maintained, makes it easier to understand that Leo's teaching includes elements that make up not only
the timeless and unchanging body of Catholic doctrine but also elements that do not. Leo taught doctrine, which by its nature does not
change, but he also addressed the specific historical circumstances that
he faced as the church's pastoral leader, and that context means some
of what he said can be dated and contingent. Discerning the difference
between these two aspects of Leo's teaching is important, and it was,

[29] Ibid., 185–86.
[30] Ibid., 146.
[31] Ibid., 151.
[32] Murray, "Leo XIII: Two Concepts of Government II," 21.

Murray clearly suggested, where people like Ottaviani and Fenton had gone wrong in their understanding of church teaching.

What Murray called "the irreducible essence of the Catholic doctrine on the Church-State relation"[33] lay in Leo's restatement of "the Gelasian thesis," the dual powers governing the temporal and spiritual aspects of human society, in opposition to "state absolutism." In that was "the absolute and final truth, in that mode of generality which alone can make the statement of the truth absolute and final, independent of historical contingencies, valid for the year 53 as for the year 1953."[34] Here we find "the central tradition . . . the two irreducible data, rational and revealed—the origin, nature, and function of civil society, and the distinct and superior origin, nature, and function of the Church. . . . Thus one comes closest to a statement of the tradition in its pure form."[35]

Leo's rejection of the separation of church and state, however, was a reaction to his particular political circumstances: the rejection of the church from all social life was the only separation of church and state that he knew. "And to the extent that this stamp is found on it, his teaching is 'dated,' and needs interpretation within the context of its own date," Murray said.[36] His rejection of religious freedom was a reaction to his particular political and social-cultural circumstances: the state had subsumed society and the people were illiterate, at the mercy of people intent on drawing them away from the moral and religious foundations of civil society, and needed the protection of government.

Murray wrote,

> The Pope himself certainly understood that he was addressing himself to a situation of historical fact; that he was proposing an immediate and practical solution to a contingent emergency; that he was not discoursing, as a political philosopher, on the rights and duties of government considered abstractly and per se. Some of his commentators have not shared this understanding. . . . An emergency existed; hence emergency measures

---

[33] Murray, "Leo XIII: Separation of Church and State," 200.
[34] Ibid., 187.
[35] Ibid., 191.
[36] Murray, "Leo XIII on Church and State," 14.

were needed. Leo XIII therefore made a practical programmatic proposal, adapted to the circumstances. He took the premise of the proposal from the political culture of his time. The premise was the society-state.[37]

---

[37] Murray, "Leo XIII: Two Concepts of Government II," 16–17.

Part Three

The Silencing of Fr. Murray

Chapter 8

Enter Ottaviani
(1953)

W hen Cardinal Alfredo Ottaviani stepped to the rostrum at Rome's prestigious Lateran University on March 2, 1953, his name was not yet the nearly household word that it would become throughout the Western world less than a decade later. But he was about to deliver a speech that exhibited the characteristics for which he would soon be well-known.

A priest of the Diocese of Rome since his ordination in 1916, Ottaviani had served in Vatican curial posts for most of the time since then. He had cofounded a scholarly journal and also penned a book on ecclesiastical law that had, since its publication in 1935, become a standard text on the subject. He had also founded an orphanage in Frascati, just outside of Rome, and was very involved in the support of another institution for poor children near the Vatican as well.[1]

In March 1953, Ottaviani was a brand new cardinal, having received the red hat from Pope Pius XII the previous January, but he was not new to his work. At the same time he made Ottaviani a cardinal, the pope had named him pro-secretary of the Holy Office—though in truth, Ottaviani had been the *de facto* head of the Vatican's important

---

[1] Joseph A. Komonchak, "Ottaviani, Alfredo, Cardinal," in *The Modern Catholic Encyclopedia,* ed. Michael Glazier and Monika Hellwig, rev. and exp. ed. (Collegeville, MN: Liturgical Press, 1994, 2004), 600–1; Michael Walsh, ed., *Dictionary of Christian Biography* (Collegeville, MN: Liturgical Press, 2001), 944; Joseph Clifford Fenton, "Cardinal Ottaviani and the Council," *AER* 148 (January 1963); Alfredo Ottaviani, *Institutiones juris publici ecclesiastici* (Romae: Typis Polyglottis Vaticanis, 1935–1936).

doctrinal congregation since 1935, when Pope Pius XI had appointed him its assessor. In short, the man who stood before that Lateran University aula on March 2, 1953, was now—with his new rank and new title—one of the most powerful men in Rome and in the global church as well. And he had been and would continue to be quite busy carrying out his duties.

Crackdown on the *Nouvelle Théologie*

Within the Catholic Church, the 1940s and 1950s had brought a renaissance of Catholic theology, following a long period of scholarly work that was too often dry, highly abstract, and inattentive to both Scripture and history. Now serious historical research among a broad range of Catholic scholars (among them Henri de Lubac, Yves Congar, Jean Danielou, Hans Urs von Balthasar, and others) had brought a strong awareness of the historical development of doctrine and the way the past formed and impacted the present. Theologians turned their attention in a new way to Scripture, the writings of the early church fathers, and the liturgical sources. Much of this work, which came to be called the *nouvelle théologie* (initially as a pejorative term), was viewed with suspicion by Vatican authorities.

In August 1950, Pope Pius XII published the encyclical *Humani Generis*, subtitled "Concerning Some False Opinions Threatening to Undermine the Foundations of Catholic Doctrine." In statements widely understood to be directed at practitioners of the *nouvelle théologie*, Pius criticized "new opinions" of theologians and made clear that God had given the authority to interpret divine revelation only to the official magisterium, "not to each of the faithful, not even to theologians." He insisted that a theologian's role was to "show how a doctrine defined by the Church is contained in the sources of revelation . . . in that sense in which it has been defined by the Church." He called for a return to the scholastic method of doing philosophy and theology.

Already in June 1950, Ottaviani's office had removed de Lubac and three other French Jesuits from their teaching positions at a historic seminary in Lyon, with all future writings to be subjected to Vatican censors before publication, due to suspicions of unorthodox teaching. The August encyclical prompted further such actions. In

February 1954, the Dominican Order, under intense pressure and threats from the Holy Office that called into question the future of the Order in France, removed three theologians—including Congar and Marie-Dominique Chenu—from teaching positions, another from editorship of a prominent publishing house, and closed down a theological journal. The move came to be known by some as "the raid on the Dominicans." For their part, Francis Connell and Joseph Fenton both emerged as prominent and staunch supporters of *Humani Generis*.

This is an important part of the context in which Murray's work, and his disputes with Fenton and Connell—both collaborators of Ottaviani—must be understood.

"Firm and Unmovable"

The March 2, 1953, event at the Lateran was to mark the anniversary of Pope Pius XII's election exactly fourteen years earlier. For the occasion, Ottaviani had prepared a major address on a topic that had become contentious throughout the Catholic world: the relationship between church and state.

"That the enemies of the Church in every time have opposed her mission," he began, "denying some—or even all—of her divine prerogatives and powers, comes as no surprise. . . . But there arises in us greater surprise, which grows into astonishment and then becomes sadness, when the attempt to snatch the weapons of justice and truth from the hands of this beneficent Mother, which is the Church, comes from her own children."

But this is precisely what was happening when Catholic scholars questioned the traditional understanding of the proper relationship between church and state. Such critics, said the cardinal, are like "the '*delicatus miles*' ['the dainty or effeminate soldier,' the Latin phrase might be translated] who wants to win without fighting."[2]

___

[2] Cardinal Alfredo Ottaviani, "Discorso di Sua Eccelenza il Cardinale Alfredo Ottaviani sul Tema 'Chiesa e Stato,'" American Catholic History Research Center and University Archives, Catholic University of America, United States Conference of Catholic Bishops Office of the General Secretary, Series 1 (General Administration Series), Box 14, Folder 12. The quotations from the speech that I offer here are my own translation from the original Italian manuscript. An English translation of the entire

Ottaviani criticized those who suggested that "among the whole body of teaching imparted by the church, it is necessary to distinguish a permanent part and a transitory part, the latter of which are said to reflect particularly temporary conditions." Those who propose such ideas refuse to take up the church's *arma veritatis* (weapon of truth). Catholics must accept all that is taught in papal encyclicals, not just what is taught infallibly—and on this topic, Ottaviani repeated Pius XII's citation, in *Humani Generis*, of Jesus: *Qui vos audit, me audit* ("Whoever hears you, you hears me").[3]

"Now, if there is a certain and incontestable truth among the general principles of Ecclesiastical Public Law," the cardinal said (mentioning the topic about which he had literally "written the book"), "it is that of the duty of those governing in a State composed almost completely of Catholics, and, consequently and consistently, governed by Catholics, to shape the legislation according to Catholic principles." It is a crime for the state to "conduct itself as though God did not exist, or as though care for religion is beyond its scope or were of no practical benefit," for society owes submission to God as much as individuals do and the government of a Catholic state must protect the religious unity of the people.[4]

"These principles," the cardinal said, "are firm and immoveable." They were true in the past, they remained true, and they would be true in the future: "and their unwavering nature—to use Dante's expression—'endures and will endure for as long as the world goes on.'"[5]

Ottaviani repeated the traditional justification for the doctrine, that error has no rights: "It is not correct to attribute the same rights to both good and evil, to truth and error." He even acknowledged the contemporary criticism of this axiom—that it is *people*, not intangible ideas like error, that are the subject of rights—responding: "It seems

---

text, commissioned from the original in March 1953 by the National Catholic Welfare Conference, is "Discourse of His Eminence Alfredo Cardinal Ottaviani on 'Church and State'" (available in the same folder of the CUA archives). An English translation of the address, with the text revised from its original delivery, was subsequently published as Ottaviani, "Church and State: Some Present Problems in Light of the Teaching of Pope Pius XII," *American Ecclesiastic Review* 128 (May 1943): 321–34.

[3] Ibid., 2.

[4] Ibid., 3.

[5] Ibid., 4.

to me, however, that the obvious truth consists rather in this: that is that the subject of the rights in question are the individual people who possess the truth, and that equal rights cannot be demanded by people on the basis of their error. . . . Only those who obey God's mandates and possess his truth and justice have true rights."[6]

After making reference to the "erroneous theories" of several European scholars, quoting their work without mentioning their names,[7] he then turned his attention to the Fenton-Murray debate, specifically mentioning Fenton by name and an article he wrote that had appeared in the June 1951 *American Ecclesiastical Review*. Ottaviani did not mention Murray's name but referred to him instead as "the proponent of the liberalizing thesis" that was so problematic. He said:

> The controversy is known which took place in the United States between two authors of opposing tendencies, whose writings were published in the *American Ecclesiastical Review*. The controversy is very well summarized by Prof. Fenton, editor of the review, in an article which appeared in the June 1951 issue. On the part of the proponent of the liberalizing thesis, the usual arguments are repeated:
>
> 1. that the State, properly speaking, cannot carry out an act of religion (for him the State is a simple symbol or a collection of institutions);
>
> 2. that "an immediate illation from the order of ethical and theological truth to the order of constitutional law, is, in principle, inadmissible" [here Ottaviani read: the words in quotes in English]. With this axiomatic language he wishes to say that the duty of the State to the worship of God can never enter into the constitutional sphere;
>
> 3. Finally, that even for a state composed of Catholics, there is no duty to profess the Catholic religion; regarding the duty to protect it, this does not become operative except in specific circumstances and precisely when the freedom of the Church cannot otherwise be guaranteed. In other

[6] Ibid., 4, 6.
[7] He quoted works by Joseph Klein, Jacques Maritain, and Robert Rouquette.

words: even in a confessional State the Church can very
well be free, without the need for relations and protections
on the part of the State as such.

It is also sad to note how the author takes exception to the
teaching of the manuals of public ecclesiastical law [and recall
here that Ottaviani himself is the author of the foremost such
manual] without taking into account that this teaching is based
in largest part on the doctrine espoused by papal documents.[8]

Significantly, Ottaviani's three-point summary of Murray's thought
was not drawn directly from Murray's own work but from Fenton's
presentation of Murray's thought in the June 1951 *AER* article, using
wording almost identical to Fenton's.[9] Note, too, the words in quotations in point 2 above. Ottaviani read these in their original English,
rather than the Italian of the rest of the speech. These are Murray's
own words from an article of his published in *AER* in May 1951.
Fenton quotes these same words, directly and critically—not once,
but twice—in the same June 1951 article that Ottaviani was citing.[10]

Before concluding his talk, Ottaviani launched into what he called
"a little 'excursus' on a practical aspect." It is ironic, he suggested, how
many of those who criticize the Catholic position on church-state relations are so little concerned with the church-state policies of the Soviet
Union, which oppresses all religion in the harshest ways. Not only that,
he said, but England, France, Switzerland, Italy, the United States, and
other nations all have various kinds of unjust legislation related to the
practice of religion within their borders, elaborating briefly on each.[11]

The church, Ottaviani concluded, would never hesitate to obey
God's command to preach the Gospel to the world, "with all the consequences that implies for man's moral conduct . . . even in political

---

[8] Ibid., 6–7.

[9] On Ottaviani's first point, see Joseph Clifford Fenton, "The Status of the Controversy," *AER* 124 (June 1951): 451–58, at 456; on his second point, see 456–57; on
his third point, see 453–54.

[10] See Fenton, "The Status of the Controversy," 456, 457. The original passage is in
John Courtney Murray, "The Problem of 'The Religion of the State,'" *AER* 124 (May
1951): 327–52, at 343.

[11] Ibid., 7–8.

life. . . . For this the church will not cease to preach, to teach, and to fight to victory."[12]

"Under Lock and Key"

Ottaviani's address caught the attention of many in Rome and beyond. Foreign diplomats to the Holy See, including those of France and Ireland, registered immediate formal protests, as did the Catholic hierarchy of Switzerland. The Vatican secretariat of state replied with embarrassment that the speech had not been an official statement and that efforts would be made to ensure that it would not be published as delivered.[13]

The National Catholic Welfare Conference (NCWC, the forerunner of the US Conference of Catholic Bishops) immediately began receiving requests for a full English translation of the talk, some of which came from editors of diocesan newspapers. And though the NCWC had indeed commissioned and received a translation, officials were wary of letting it go public.[14]

The director of the NCWC press office provided copies of the original Italian text to both Fenton and Connell in response to their request, but others, like the young Fr. Frederick McManus (who in 1953 still had a long and remarkable scholarly and pastoral career ahead of him) were rebuffed. Once the English translation became available, the NCWC hoped to limit its distribution only to those diocesan paper editors who were especially persistent in their requests, and even then only after insisting that their diocesan bishops approve its use. The press office

[12] Ibid., 9.

[13] Joseph A. Komonchak, "The Silencing of John Courtney Murray," in *Cristianesimo nella storia: Saggi in onore di Giuseppe Alberigo*, ed. Alberto Melloni, et al. (Bologna: Il Mulino, 1996), 657–702, at 670. Komonchak provides citations of the diplomatic documentation. He also notes that the American Embassy in Rome did not lodge a similar protest. Murray mentions the protests of the Swiss hierarchy, as well as the French and Irish diplomats, in his talk of March 25, 1954.

[14] Frank A. Hall to Monsignor Howard J. Carroll correspondence, March 20, 1953. Hall to Carroll correspondence, March 27, 1953. American Catholic History Research Center and University Archives, The Catholic University of America, United States Conference of Catholic Bishops Office of the General Secretary, Series 1 (General Administration Series), box 14, folder 12.

director worried in an internal memo that one editor "clearly is itching to bring out precisely the things that it is thought unwise to bring out," noting that he kept his copies of Ottaviani's speech "under lock and key."[15]

Cardinal Spellman shared a copy of the speech with the rector of New York's archdiocesan seminary. "I think you will be interested in reading this," he said in an accompanying letter, then added that "Archbishop O'Boyle and myself saw no useful purpose in having it published in The Ecclesiastical Review."[16]

Ottaviani himself was not so reticent about the speech's distribution, nor was Fenton. On the same day he delivered it, Ottaviani sent a copy by personal messenger to the Washington-based National Catholic News Service's Rome correspondent. Fenton quickly sought and received Ottaviani's permission to print it in *AER*, which he did in the May issue, but the text that was published there was significantly revised, shortened, and toned down, probably by the cardinal himself.

Murray's initial reaction to the Ottaviani talk came in a private March 24 letter to Fenton. He charged Fenton with misrepresenting his views, which had led to Ottaviani's doing the same. He also made reference to untrue "rumors" that he had heard were circulating about himself around the Catholic University campus, insisting that Fenton correct them there. "It is neither easy nor pleasant to answer the letter you wrote me a week ago," Fenton replied on March 31. He denied any awareness of rumors about Murray and also denied that either he or Ottaviani had misrepresented Murray's thought.[17]

Fenton sent Murray a second, longer, and more conciliatory letter on April 4, the day before Easter, "to try to clear up some misunderstandings and thus to prevent or to destroy some attitudes incompatible with what should be our mutual priestly amor fraternitatis." Murray responded on April 11, saying he was distressed by their conflict, ac-

[15] Hall to Carroll correspondence, March 20, 1953.

[16] Spellman to Msgr. Fearns, March 31, 1953, archives of the Archdiocese of New York, St. Joseph's Seminary, Dunwoodie, To Cardinal Spellman—Apostolic Delegate to the United States, S/D-3, folder 6.

[17] Fenton to Murray correspondence, March 31, 1953, John Courtney Murray Papers, box 1, folder 70, Georgetown University Library, Special Collections Research Center, Washington, DC. (The March 24 letter is missing, but the following letter from Fenton, of April 4, mentions the March 24 date.)

knowledging he had been abrupt and careless, and concluding, "If my letter was hurtful, I offer you my apologies." In an April 17 letter, Fenton, now addressing Murray as "John" rather than as "Father Murray" as in the previous letters, expressed hope that they could get together in person. "It will be a pleasure to sit around and laugh at a correspondence which, in retrospect, looks anything but edifying or even serious." Though both make reference to their hopes of getting together in a couple of further letters, their correspondence ends soon after that, and the get-together, it seems, never happened.[18]

For months the speech was a matter of discussion among theologians and church leaders; some were pleased by it, but many, more discretely, were critical. In fact, it was somewhat commonly understood in clerical circles around Rome that the pope himself disapproved of the aggressive tone and unnuanced nature of the Lateran address. During one of his many business trips to Rome, Joseph Fenton wrote in his journal of a conversation he had with a professor of archeology at Rome's Pontifical Biblical Institute, who told him that "the Pope was displeased with Ottaviani."[19]

For his part, Murray was careful to seek confirmation that Ottaviani's views did not represent a formal statement of the magisterium. He received it from highly trustworthy sources. Pius XII's personal secretary, Robert Leiber, SJ, who was well-known as a trusted associate of the pope, wrote in a letter to Murray in June:

> About the conference of Cardinal Ottaviani: You know and you can use it, it only represents the private views of the Cardinal. It has no official or semi-official character. Your Reverence would do well, in my humble opinion, at least in a personal letter to the Cardinal, to correct what he erroneously characterizes as your opinion. You would do well to leave out of this matter the personal qualities of Msgr. Fenton.[20]

[18] Fenton to Murray, April 4, 1953; Murray to Fenton, April 1, 1953; Fenton to Murray, April 17, 1953. All these are from John Courtney Murray Papers, Box 1, Folder 70.

[19] Fenton journal, "Ninth Trip to Rome, May 1954–June 1955," June 13, 1954, box 1, folder 3, available at http://doc.wrlc.org/handle/2041/112120.

[20] June 12, 1953, cited in Donald E. Pelotte, *John Courtney Murray: Theologian in Conflict* (New York: Paulist Press, 1975), 64n44.

Perhaps even more significant was Leiber's statement in the same letter that the pope had expressed his "disagreement" with Ottaviani's approach.[21]

A few months later, on November 16, the topic of the Ottaviani speech came up in conversation as Murray was having dinner with Cardinal Samuel Stritch, who was archbishop of Chicago, and Cardinal Edward Mooney, the archbishop of Detroit. The previous month, Stritch had given a talk, in the presence of the pope, on the occasion of the dedication of the new North American College (the Amerian Seminary in Rome), during which he had made reference to the importance of freedom in the founding of the United States. At the November dinner, Stritch told Murray that he had been assured by Monsignor Giovanni Battista Montini—another close associate of the pope's (who was in fact just weeks away from being named the archbishop of Milan and less than a decade from his own election to the papacy)—that Ottaviani's address had been "purely private utterance."[22]

Still, with the head of the Holy Office publicly criticizing Murray's work at a time when the same office had been taking serious steps against other theologians and movements, the writing was already on the wall. On November 15, 1953, Fr. Vincent McCormick, the American assistant at the Jesuit generalate in Rome, wrote to John J. McMahon, Murray's provincial, "I think the time has come for Fr. Murray to put down in simple, clear statements his full, present position regarding this Church-State question and send it to me for Father General. Sic mandatum [Thus is the command]."[23]

---

[21] Pelotte, *John Courtney Murray*, 47. At this writing, I have not personally viewed the Leiber letter, presently in the Georgetown archives. Pelotte quotes Leiber saying the Ottaviani talk did not represent an official statement of the Holy See (Pelotte, 37) and quotes Murray's notes asserting that Leiber said the pope disagreed with the statement (Pelotte, 47). Pelotte seems to presume that Leiber expressed Pius's disagreement, but his account leaves open the possibility that Murray *inferred* (perhaps mistakenly) from Leiber's words that the pope disagreed with Ottaviani.

[22] Pelotte, *John Courtney Murray*, 40 (incl. n54).

[23] Pelotte, *John Courtney Murray*, 39n53.

Chapter 9

The Pope Speaks,
Murray Seals His Fate
(1953–1954)

O n December 6, 1953—nine months after Cardinal Ottaviani's Lateran address and just as the fourth of Murray's five
"Leo" articles appeared in *Theological Studies*—Pope Pius
XII received the members of the Union of Catholic Jurists, who were
meeting in Rome for their national convention, in an audience. One
might reasonably have expected the pope's comments on such an occasion to have been relatively pro forma. But the address he delivered
that day proved to be quite significant to the debate in which Murray,
Fenton, and now Ottaviani were hotly engaged. It came to be known
as *Ci Riesce* (pronounced *chee ree-AY-shay*), for the first two words of
the Italian text.[1]

Pius's *Ci Riesce*

The pope opened his talk by noting that the relationships among the
world's community of nations were "growing in multiplicity and inten-
sity" and that the development of a more formal international structure,
a "supranational juridical community," was therefore likely.[2] (We should
recall here that, in 1953, the United Nations organization was less than
a decade old and construction of its impressive headquarters building
in New York City had been completed only the previous year.)

---

[1] Pius XII, "The Discourse *'Ci Riesce'*," *AER* 130 (February 1954): 129–38.
[2] Ibid., 129–30.

The pope spoke positively about such a possibility but pointed out that it would raise the complicated question of "the practical coexistence [*convivenza*] of Catholic and non-Catholic states." Since such an international community in modern times would surely allow citizens the free exercise of their religion, the question that arose "for the jurist, the statesman, and the Catholic state" was whether they could cooperate with and implicitly approve such arrangements by formally entering this organization of nations. Would "toleration" be permissible? Or is "positive repression" of religious beliefs other than Catholic ones "always a duty" for rulers of "Catholic states"?[3]

Pius answered the question by posing another question:

> Could God, although it would be possible and easy for Him to repress error and moral deviation, in some cases choose the "non impedire" [not to impede] without contradicting His infinite perfection? Could it be that *in certain circumstances* He would not give men any mandate, would not impose any duty, and would not even communicate the right to impede or to repress what is erroneous and false? A look at things as they are gives as affirmative answer. Reality shows that error and sin are in the world in great measure. God reprobates them, but He permits them to exist. Hence the affirmation, "religious and moral error must always be impeded, when it is possible, because toleration of them is in itself immoral," is not valid *absolutely and unconditionally.*

> Moreover, God has not given even to human authority such an absolute and universal command in matters of faith and morality. . . . The duty of repressing moral and religious error cannot therefore be an ultimate norm of action. It must be subordinate to *higher and more general* norms, which *in some circumstances* permit, and perhaps even seem to indicate as the better policy, toleration of error in order to promote *a greater good.*[4]

---

[3] Ibid., 132–33.

[4] Ibid., 134. Italics in the original. I have adjusted the punctuation slightly to make the text more clear.

The conclusion, said the pope, is that Catholic leaders must keep in mind two principles as they approached the possibility of joining whatever formal community of nations might develop. First, "that which does not correspond to truth or to the norm of morality has no right to exist." Second, allowing such error to exist by civil law "can nevertheless be justified in the interests of a higher and more general good." And so while "in principle, that is, in theory, [the church] cannot approve complete separation of [church and state]," she can and sometimes does tolerate it.[5]

Differing Takes

Both Murray and Fenton saw *Ci Riesce* as a vindication of their own positions—or least they presented it as though it was.

Less than a week after the papal address, Murray had as yet seen only a summary of the full text, but he was convinced that it was "clearly the Pope's own reply to the famous discourse of Cardinal Ottaviani [of March 2, 1953]. And it is an important disavowal of the position taken by the latter." Writing to his friend, the renowned church historian John Tracy Ellis, he said, "It will be interesting to see what our fellow editor [Fenton] will have to say" about it.[6] Ellis agreed with Murray's take and reported to him a conversation he'd had with a noted French Dominican scholar who also saw the talk as "a reversal of the Ottaviani thesis."[7]

The noted Jesuit scholar Gustave Weigel, one of Murray's colleagues on the faculty at Woodstock, understood the papal address similarly. In a December 16 Vatican Radio interview, Weigel said that the "lofty doctrine" offered in *Ci Riesce* would be "enthusiastically received by all men of good will." He continued:

> It certainly clarifies the obscurities lurking in the minds of so many of our non-Catholic brethren who feel that the Catholic Church is a conspiracy to rob them of their right to follow

---

[5] Ibid., 134–35, 137–38.

[6] Donald E. Pelotte, *John Courtney Murray: Theologian in Conflict* (New York: Paulist Press, 1975), 43.

[7] Ibid., 44–45.

conscience in their religious decisions. . . . Above all, it will end
the accusation of not a few who assert that the Catholic Church
has a double norm for solving Church-State relationships. According to the accusation the Church demands liberty for personal religious belief in countries where Catholics constitute a
minority, while Catholic uniformity is imposed on all citizens in
lands where Catholics form a political majority. The doctrine of
the Pope is wholly different, for he speaks of a tolerant worldwide society formed by individual sovereign states, Catholic and
non-Catholic, which will govern in their own communities in
accord with the principles obtaining in the total world federation.
This, according to the Pope, is in thorough harmony with the
abiding doctrine of the Catholic Church.[8]

Fenton put a very different spin on the talk. The *American Ecclesiastical Review* published an English translation of Pius's address in its
February issue, accompanied by an article by Fenton that claimed the
pope had vindicated the thesis-hypothesis approach. Calling *Ci Reice*
"one of the most important pontifical statements of recent times,"
Fenton pointed out that the pope had taught that a ruler does not
always have a duty to repress error, which implies, of course, that the
same ruler sometimes *does* have such a right. If the ruler ought not to
repress error under certain circumstances, Fenton said, then obviously
there are also circumstances in which he ought to.[9]

Fenton said the pope's teaching was founded on the very vocabulary
and ideas that Murray had repeatedly rejected. Pius had said that the
church cannot approve the complete separation of church and state
"in principle or as a thesis,"[10] thus making explicit reference to the
standard thesis-hypothesis distinction, while Murray had denied the
validity of structuring the argument in those terms. The pope had also

---

[8] Weigel's Vatican Radio address was published as "Religious Toleration in a
World Society," *America* 90 (January 9, 1954): 376.

[9] Joseph Clifford Fenton, "The Teachings of the *Ci Riesce*," *AER* 130 (February
1953): 117.

[10] The Italian phrase of the pope's original text was *"per principio, ossia in tesi."*
The NCWC translated this as "in principle, that is, in theory," while Fenton rendered
it "in principle or as a thesis." Both translations are viable ones.

made reference to "Catholic states" and "non-Catholic states," more terminology that Murray had rejected as inappropriate to modern circumstances. Finally, the pope had stated rather clearly that error has no rights. And so, Fenton wrote with a flourish, "we can expect that, in the future, there will be no objections" to such terminology or teaching.[11]

Murray Seals His Fate

While Fenton's article on *Ci Riesce* had appeared just a few weeks after Pope Pius had delivered the talk, Murray said little publicly about the speech for the better part of a year. That changed on March 25, 1954, when he delivered an address at The Catholic University of America. If Fenton had taken out his guns in the *AER* article, Murray had a few rounds himself to fire.

Standing before a crowded room at CUA's McMahon Hall, Murray began by saying that *Ci Riesce* was "important" and an "encouragement and satisfaction to me." The teaching the pope offered in the address, he said, "represents doctrinal progress" and a "development of doctrine."[12]

He then commented that the address "is [the] Pope's public correction of impressions left by C[ardinal] Ottaviani's construction of Catholic doctrine" in his address on church and state at the Lateran the previous year, a correction that the Holy Father had offered in "all gentleness." Murray mentioned the objections voiced to the Vatican by the various diplomats in the wake of Ottaviani's speech, and he also said the speech had "evoked disagreement on doctrinal grounds in high Roman circles; in [the] Pope's entourage; [and] in [the] mind of [the] Pope himself." For this reason, Murray said, Pope Pius had "sought [an] occasion" to set the record straight and had "carefully prepared" for the address to the Italian jurists in order to do just that.[13]

[11] Ibid., 120–23.

[12] John Courtney Murray, "Notes from which Fr. Murray spoke in McMahon Hall, Catholic University, March 25, 1954," (hereafter, "Notes"), 1. A full text or transcription of Murray's March 25, 1954, address does not exist. Murray spoke from handwritten notes, which he transcribed into a nine-page single-spaced typescript following the talk. Both documents are available in the CUA archives. The quotations here are from Murray's typescript.

[13] Ibid.

These comments were a departure from Murray's customary tactful demeanor. Though they came in the first minutes of his address, he had probably already said enough to provoke the swift reaction from Rome that his words would soon receive.[14]

The conclusion to be drawn from the papal address, Murray said, were that "appeal to Ottaviani" on the question of church and state ought henceforth to be "cautious and discriminating." Anyone who holds a theory about religious freedom that resembles Cardinal Ottaviani's was now "under necessity of revising his views."[15] Murray allowed, however, that the problem was not primarily with Ottaviani. It was the current theory, the received opinion. *Ci Riesce* served to make clear several faults in that theory.[16]

First, the received opinion conceives of the question too narrowly. It limits the question to a matter of national sovereignty, whereas Pope Pius made clear in his talk that "national good is not the highest good," but that both the good of the universal church—including its ability to live a "free and peaceful life amid divided humanity"—and the good of the international community are both more important.[17]

Second, the received opinion is based on a faulty method, one that is "excessively, almost exclusively juridical." In contrast, the Holy Father insisted on the primacy of a theological method and also employed a historical one. Regarding the latter, the pope recognized, Murray said, that the church must either keep pace with historical developments or risk irrelevance. "All development of doctrine in this field," he said, "[is] occasioned by history."[18]

---

[14] Komonchak notes that Murray "indulged in some humorous and disparaging remarks about Ottaviani himself" (Joseph A. Komonchak, "'The Crisis in Church-State Relationships in the U.S.A.': A Recently Discovered Text by John Courtney Murray," *The Review of Politics* 61, no. 4 [Autumn 1999]: 675–714, at 684). It is unclear to me whether Komonchak is referring to the comments noted here, or if perhaps Murray, in his spoken address, made further, more personal comments that he did not include in his typescript.

[15] Murray, "Notes," 1.

[16] Ibid., 1–2.

[17] Ibid., 2.

[18] Ibid., 2–4.

Third, the received opinion fails to account for and balance all of the principles most relevant to this discussion. It is a question "of emphases" and "of 'style' of theory."[19]

Fourth, the received opinion, as a result of the third fault above, is a "defective and . . . untrue" systematization of the tradition.[20]

Pius XII, Murray said, "dismantles" the logic of the received tradition, "piece by piece, at the same time that he reaffirms the tradition of which this theory unsuccessfully pretends to be a construction." He did this by teaching that error need not always be repressed by a ruler, that there are higher goods and norms than repressing error, and that there are circumstances in which a ruler ought not to repress error or might not even have the right to do it. "Thus a particular theory is dismantled. Whatever its simplicity and pretended logic, it is not Catholic thesis, not valid construction of tradition, not doctrine but doctrinaire theorizing."[21]

Murray concluded that Pius XII had, in *Ci Riesce*, decisively rejected the thesis-hypothesis theory of church-state relations. He "maintains that both intolerance and tolerance are hypotheses." No longer could Spain's establishment of Catholicism as the national religion be regarded as the "thesis" and the United States' religious freedom as one "hypothesis." "Both are hypotheses; each to be judged on its own merits within its own circumstances."[22]

While one might have been able to draw the thesis-hypothesis theory from a reading of Leo XIII's *Libertas*, Murray said, after *Ci Riesce*, that was no longer possible. "Pius XII, today, speaks the tradition; [the] construction he rejects was never more than 'received opinion'; now not to be received."[23]

"For the Protection of the Truth"

The lecture made a splash on the CUA campus and was the topic of much discussion among the theology faculty and students. John Tracy Ellis, who called the address "splendid in every way, a true university

19 Ibid., 4.
20 Ibid.
21 Ibid., 4–6.
22 Ibid., 7–9.
23 Ibid., 7.

performance," noted to Murray that it had "stirred a great deal of discussion on the campus."[24] Presciently, he warned Murray to "hold yourself to a reasonable pace now so that you may be with us for a long time to come."[25]

But not everyone shared Ellis's enthusiasm of the lecture, and giving a talk that took direct aim at Ottaviani on Connell and Fenton's home turf was poking the alligator with a stick. Both scholars immediately sent off letters describing the address to Ottaviani's office in Rome, as did Fr. Maurice Sheehy, another CUA professor and friend of Fenton's.[26]

In a March 27 reply to Connell, Cardinal Ottaviani wrote, "I have concluded that it is my duty to act . . . for the protection of the truth and for the defense of Catholic thought. Also, patience and charity have limits in the light of justice and truth."[27]

On April 1, 1954—only one week after the CUA lecture—Cardinal Ottaviani wrote a letter to Cardinal Spellman in New York. Though this letter is missing from the archival records in which it is registered as being stored, we get a good sense of its contents from the response that Cardinal Spellman mailed back to Ottaviani on April 5. Spellman assured Ottaviani that he would take up the matter with the rector of CUA. He added, "I would appreciate it if you will give me more details of what Father Murray said in his lecture that was offensive to you and just what quotation he made from any address of His Holiness and what interpretations were given to the words of our Holy Father."[28]

Fenton criticized Murray's talk in the May issue of *AER*. He wrote that Ottaviani's position, which Murray had criticized, was "simply

---

[24] Pelotte, *John Courtney Murray*, 47. Fenton also acknowledged, in his personal journal, the wide attention Murray's talk was receiving at CUA, but more negatively, referring to "the bad feeling [it] had engendered at the University." See Fenton journal, "Ninth Trip to Rome, May 1954–June 1955," June 13, 1954, box 1, folder 3, available at http://doc.wrlc.org/handle/2041/112120.

[25] Pelotte, *John Courtney Murray*, 47.

[26] Komonchak, "The Crisis in Church-State Relationships in the U.S.A.," 684.

[27] Joseph A. Komonchak, "The Silencing of John Courtney Murray," in *Cristianesimo nella storia: Saggi in onore di Giuseppe Alberigo*, ed. Alberto Melloni, et al. (Bologna: Il Mulino, 1996), 657–702, at 677.

[28] Spellman to Ottaviani, April 5, 1954, NY Archdiocesan Archives.

what is contained and what has been contained in the great body of manuals in theology and in public ecclesiastical law which deal with this particular subject, the teaching of the magisterium itself."[29] The following issue of *AER* had another article critical of Murray's CUA address, this time by Msgr. Giuseppe de Meglio, an official of the Holy Office, who suggested the talk had been a personal attack on the cardinal.[30]

On the other hand, there was talk among Vatican cognoscenti that the pope had made private comments in defense of Murray. In June, during one of his many visits to Rome, Fenton heard of it from Robert North, SJ, a professor of archeology at Rome's prestigious Pontifical Biblical Institute. North, Fenton journaled, "told me about the sentiment of the Pope, and about a statement which the Pope is said to have made to the effect that Murray was within his rights."[31]

If this were the case, Fenton disapproved of the pope's theology. He wrote:

> Apparently the Pope *as a private theologian* does approve of Murray or at least is not unsympathetic with him. But, this is not a doctrine which he attempts to teach or to support, even in his capacity as a private theologian. On the other hand, the one authoritative statement which has come from him [the *Ci Riesce* address] has upheld the Ottaviani thesis. There is a parallel in the case of Pius XI. According to [name illegible], our old rector, the old man held some weird opinions as a personal theologian. The Pius XII case seems to be a case in which the divine protection of Catholic doctrine has become, for all intents and purposes, visible.[32]

[29] Joseph Clifford Fenton, "Toleration and the Church-State Controversy," *AER* 130 (May 1954): 342–43.

[30] "*Ci Riesce* and Cardinal Ottaviani's Discourse," *AER* 130 (June 1954): 384–87.

[31] Fenton journal, "Ninth Trip to Rome, May 1954–June 1955," June 13, 1954, box 1, folder 3, available at http://doc.wrlc.org/handle/2041/112120.

[32] Ibid. Emphasis in the original.

Chapter 10

"You May Write Poetry"
(1954–1958)

B y the summer of 1954, Francis Connell had already been calling
for public repudiation of Murray's views in private letters to
Cardinal Ottaviani and other curial cardinals for at least four
years. Joseph Fenton, Murray's staunchest theological foe, clearly had
Ottaviani's ear. And Ottaviani himself had singled out Murray for
criticism in his high profile March 1953 Lateran address. In addition
to that, several articles published in the semiofficial Vatican journal
Civiltà Cattolica between 1950 and 1952 had also leveled criticism at
the views Murray espoused, without mentioning him by name.[1]

In the meantime, Pius XII's encyclical *Humani Generis* had been
published in August 1950. February 1954 had brought the Vatican's
new disciplinary "raid on the Dominicans" mentioned above, and
other noted theologians, like Jean Daniélou and Henri Bouillard, also
lived during this time under the shadow of suspicion by doctrinal
authorities.[2] As a result, there was no misunderstanding in anyone's

---

[1] Joseph A. Komonchak, "Religious Freedom and the Confessional State: The
Twentieth Century Discussion," *Revue d'Histoire Ecclésiastique* 95 (2000): 634–50,
at 646–47.

[2] An episode offered by Pelotte provides an idea of the environment of the times:
In August 1954, the highly regarded church historian John Tracy Ellis was invited to
deliver a lecture at the Tenth International Congress of Historical Sciences in Rome in
the following year. Out of courtesy, Ellis sought the permission of his bishop, Cardinal
O'Boyle. O'Boyle refused permission, noting, "you know there is Monsignor Fenton,
the *AER*, and all that sort of thing" (Donald E. Pelotte, *John Courtney Murray: Theologian in Conflict* [New York: Paulist Press, 1975], 50).

90

mind where the critical attention to Murray's work on the part of the Holy Office might lead.

"Two There Are . . ."

In the spring of 1954, Murray made his case again. He did it this time by contributing a chapter to a book of collected essays published by the University of Notre Dame Press called *The Catholic Church in World Affairs* (hereafter, *CCWA*).[3] In it, Murray repeated his arguments about the Gelasian principle of the two powers, "characterized by a primacy of the spiritual over the political," and rejected any "monism" that submerged the state into the church or the church into the state.[4]

Historically, Murray argued, the church has insisted on the dualism, in large part to protect its own freedom to carry out its mission authentically:

> She does indeed always fight under the same banner on which is emblazoned the pregnant device of Gelasius: "Two there are . . ." And the stake in the struggle is always the same—the freedom of the Church to dispense the sacred things—in brief, the Word and the sacraments—committed to her charge; and the freedom of the human spirit as anchored to the inviolability from political profanation of the sacred things in the temporal order.[5]

History, Murray wrote, was dotted by various efforts to reduce the "two powers" to one: royal absolutism in the seventeenth and eighteenth centuries, French republicanism in the nineteenth, and totalitarianism in the twentieth. Because the nature of governments change, so must the church's stance toward them, like a wrestler grappling with an opponent, countering hold with hold.[6] And so the church's relationship with the state characterized by a constitutional government

---

[3] John Courtney Murray, "On the Structure of the Church-State Problem," in *The Catholic Church in World Affairs*, ed. Waldemar Gurian and M. A. Fitzsimons (Notre Dame, IN: University of Notre Dame Press, 1954), 11–32.

[4] Ibid., 11.

[5] Ibid., 16.

[6] Ibid., 17.

representing the people must be different than it was when the state was essentially a king with absolute power.

Murray also repeated his arguments about the historical context of the thesis-antithesis theory within "the rationalist theory of the absolutely autonomous freedom of human reason as the single architect of all order."[7] To this, the church rightly responded with "an absolute, total, and uncompromising protest against the infringement of her freedom and the politicization of her sacred things . . . [and] equally absolute opposition to the idea behind the state monism."[8] But the church had pushed that stance a bit too far, so that "the absolute doctrinal opposition to the rationalist premises of 'the modern liberties' carried over . . . to a disapproval of these 'modern liberties' as political institutions."

In the twentieth century, the experience of totalitarianism had put the same freedoms in a new light. And so the church's openness to these freedoms is not to be considered "a belated making peace with the rationalism of the Enlightenment," but rather

> a question of disengaging the concept of democracy as a political system from its rationalist premises. . . . It is a question of showing that the "modern freedoms" as political institutions are as capable of projection from right as from wrong premises, and that this is true also of freedom of religion as a political principle, resting on a sound political theory of the limitations of governmental power.[9]

In this situation, Murray said, "the thesis-hypothesis disjunction . . . is no longer particularly useful."[10]

"There Are People after My Head"

Fenton took all this as a direct and intolerable rejection of Catholic doctrine that Ottaviani had articulated so clearly at the Lateran the previous year. Fenton's personal journal during a May–June 1954 visit to Rome reveals that Ottaviani was at the time assigning him reports on

[7] Ibid., 21.
[8] Ibid., 22.
[9] Ibid., 29.
[10] Ibid., 30.

Murray and his place in the US ecclesial landscape. Fenton approached the task enthusiastically and personally handed the reports over to the cardinal. Fenton's journals include copious notes to himself in preparation for these reports, though he often coded them to varying degrees, referring to Murray as "Z" and Ottaviani as "the boss" and "the old man." (By 1956, he was also referring to Ottaviani as "Uncle.") A draft of a long and critical analysis for Ottaviani of the Murray *CCWA* chapter is disguised as notes for an article. He concludes it: "With this in mind, I come to my recommendation. Regretfully and after prayerful consideration, I consider it my duty to recommend that Z's article be condemned *nominatem* by the Cath[olic] public."[11]

Having submitted this report (of twenty-five double-spaced pages) in person to Ottaviani's office on June 10,[12] Fenton journaled that he again "ended up with the boss, who asked me for another report," this one on the topic of the landscape of the American hierarchy with regard to Murray and the religious freedom debate. "I must do everything within my power," Fenton wrote, "to make this most recently requested report as accurate and complete as possible. . . . I shall discuss a fact, the background of that fact, and the steps which should, in my opinion, be taken to alleviate the intolerably bad situation now existing."[13] The subsequent notes are also coded, referring to the US bishops as "members of the board of directors," particular bishops with all sorts of codenames, the United States as "Norway," and Ottaviani as "X." A major portion of these notes are about the attitudes of the current US bishops toward Ottaviani and Fenton's recommendation that several new bishops, especially supportive of him, be named—in a process that sidesteps the typical procedures for determining such appointments—to key posts in the United States. "The appointment of 2 or 3 men attached to X *immediately* would be, for the Norwegian people and in their eyes, the clearest-cut victory for X now possible. . . . The men selected . . . should be good entertainers and should be in positions where they can entertain."[14]

[11] Fenton journal, "Ninth Trip to Rome, May 1954–June 1955," June 7, 1954, box 1, folder 3, available at http://doc.wrlc.org/handle/2041/112120.

[12] Ibid., June 11, 1954.

[13] Ibid., June 14, 1954.

[14] Ibid.

Fenton delivered this second report to the Holy Office on June 15, then left Rome to return to the United States the following day. On the trip home, he wrote in his journal:

> In one way the trip was much more successful than I had any reason to imagine it could be. There is a good chance that I have taken a leading part in an action which may turn out to be one of the most important in the history of the Catholic Church in the USA. . . . There seems to be ample evidence over here that the big boys are working in the right direction. . . . Unquestionably when I was asked to make report #2, I came closer to influencing the activity of the Congregation than I ever dreamed I could.[15]

Four "Errors"

Fenton's reports were included in a formal evaluation of Murray's *CCWA* chapter conducted by the Holy Office. This process concluded on July 7, 1954, and resulted in the identification of four doctrinal errors in the work. The four errors attributed to Murray and condemned by the Holy Office were described in the Holy Office report as follows:

(a.) The Catholic confessional State, professing itself as such, is not an ideal to which organized political society is universally obliged.

(b.) Full religious liberty can be considered as a valid political ideal in a truly democratic State.

(c.) The State organized on a genuinely democratic basis must be considered to have done its duty when it has guaranteed the freedom of the Church by a general guarantee of liberty of religion.

(d.) It is true that Leo XIII has said *civitas . . . debent eum in colendo numine morem usurpare modumque quo coli se Deus ipse demonstravit velle* [states must follow that way of worshipping the divinity which God himself has shown that he desires] (Enc.

[15] Ibid., June 19, 1954.

Immortale Dei). Words such as these can be understood as referring to the State considered as organized on a basis other than that of the perfectly democratic State but to this latter strictly speaking are not applicable.[16]

As Joseph Komonchak's helpful research indicates, none of the four propositions are taken directly from the *CCWA* article. The first can be recognized in a 1949 article by Murray; the second and third seem to be taken from Murray's 1950 memo to Msgr. Giovanni Battista Montini, the Vatican secretariat of state official (and later pope); and the fourth is not clearly from any particular writing, though it may represent a summary statement of Murray's thinking. In short, the *CCWA* article was more the occasion used for the action against Murray than the actual work in question. The situation, then, was that a private memo Murray has written for Montini's personal use became—though Montini himself probably did not foresee it when he provided a copy to the Holy Office—a crucial part of the Holy Office's efforts formally to judge Murray's work, a judgment that resulted in his being silenced by his Jesuit superiors.[17]

On July 26, 1954, Murray's superior general, Christopher O'Toole, received a letter from Cardinal Giuseppe Pizzardo, secretary of the Holy Office and prefect of the Congregation for Seminaries and Universities, demanding that the errors proposed by Murray be corrected in an insert to be included in any further copies of the book to be sold.[18] Murray learned of the judgments against his work in August.

"There are people who are after my head," Murray wrote in a September 13, 1954, letter to M. A. Fitzsimons, who had coedited *CCWA*.

[16] Ibid., October 28, 1954. Joseph A. Komonchak translates the Latin of the quotation from Leo: "states must follow that way of worshipping the divinity which God himself has shown that he desires" ("'The Crisis in Church-State Relationships in the U.S.A.': A Recently Discovered Text by John Courtney Murray," *The Review of Politics* 61 (1999): 674–714, at 684–85).

[17] Komonchak, "The Crisis in Church-State Relationships in the U.S.A.," 685.

[18] Joseph A. Komonchak, "The Silencing of John Courtney Murray," in *Cristianesimo nella storia: Saggi in onore di Giuseppe Alberigo*, ed. Alberto Melloni (Bologna: Il Mulino, 1996), 657–702, at 682.

> I had a private communication from my Father General in
> Rome to this effect. He is concerned about my head, and quite
> sympathetic. . . . I seem presently to be caught in a rather
> taut Roman situation. For my part, I believe and hope that it
> will resolve itself in a manner favorable to me and my friends.
> But for the moment one treads on the well-known eggs. . . .
> I have a price on my head.[19]

Both Fenton and Connell received copies of the list from the Vatican, but the condemnation was never made public, a fact that caused Fenton much frustration. Indeed, the frequency with which he transcribed these four points verbatim into his personal journal over the following decade—in October 1954, March 1957, November 1960, and March 1962 (!)[20]—suggests he was quite preoccupied by them. More than two years after the Holy Office's judgment against Murray, Fenton was still insisting to the highest Vatican officials on the need to publicize it. "No purpose is served if this teaching is known by only two priests, both of whom are teaching at the university," he told Cardinal Pizzardo in a personal conversation. "In the meantime, M[urray] is continually in the public eye, and is being represented as the great American theologian. It would seem best to publicize this teaching at once."[21] He privately expressed his ongoing frustration in March 1962, writing (after repeating the four points): "There has never been anything less effective in the Church than the secret condemnation of an error."[22]

[19] Pelotte, *John Courtney Murray*, 67n83.

[20] Fenton journals: "Ninth Trip to Rome, May 1954–June 1955," October 25, 1954; "My Tenth Trip to Rome, also the Eleventh, Twelfth, and Thirteenth Trips, August 1955–September 1958," box 1, folder 4, available at http://doc.wrlc.org/handle /2041/112121, March 2, 1957; "Notes of My Previous Fourteenth Trip to Rome, November 18, 1960–December 12, 1960," box 1, folder 6, available at http://doc.wrlc .org/handle/2041/112123, November 18, 1960; and "Journal of the Sixteenth, Seventeenth, Eighteenth, and Nineteenth Trips to Rome, March 1962–February 1963," box 1, folder 9, available at http://doc.wrlc.org/handle/2041/112136), March 16, 1962.

[21] Fenton journal, "My Tenth Trip to Rome," September 6, 1956.

[22] Fenton journal, "Journal of the Sixteenth, Seventeenth, Eighteenth, and Nineteenth Trips to Rome, March 1962–February 1963," March 16, 1962.

Silenced

Either at the same time Murray was informed of the Holy Office's judgment against his work or, it seems more likely, sometime later, Murray was instructed that all of his writings would have to be approved by censors at the Jesuit Curia in Rome prior to publication. The exact timing is unclear due to lack of archival evidence; there does not seem to be reference to the involvement of censors in the extant correspondence, both official and personal, in the summer and fall of 1954, but Murray was certainly submitting his work for approval to Rome by February 1955.[23]

On July 9, 1955, Vincent McCormick, SJ, an American assistant at the Jesuit generalate in Rome, had the task of reporting to Murray that what was to have been the sixth and final installment of his series of *Theological Studies* articles on Pope Leo XIII had been refused permission for publication by the Roman censors. Assuring Murray that "these men have your interests at heart," McCormick quoted the censor, who commented in Latin: "The text cannot be published; the author has been accused recently by his 'friends' in America and here in Rome to the Holy Office. Nevertheless, there are not a few things in the manuscript that are expressed very well."[24]

"It seems to me," McCormick concluded to Murray, "a mistake to wish to carry on with that controverted question under present circumstances." Seeing no wisdom in "provoking those who will not be appeased," he said, "Fr. General agrees with the final verdict, although not with every comment of the censors. . . . So, fiat. Time will bring changes."[25]

Murray responded to McCormick's letter on Friday, July 15, thanking him for his "delicate way of saying, 'You're through!'"[26] By Monday, Murray had collected from his room all of the books related to the topic of church and state that belonged to the CUA library and returned them.[27]

[23] See Pelotte, *John Courtney Murray*, 52.
[24] Ibid. (My translation from the Latin.)
[25] Ibid.
[26] Ibid., 53.
[27] Ibid., 69n95.

Later in the year, Murray began inquiring to McCormick what sort of topics he *could* write on. In a mid-December letter, McCormick promised to pass the question on to the superior general. Meanwhile, he wrote, "I suppose you may write poetry. Between harmless poetry and Church-State problems, what fields are taboo I don't know; but ordinary prudence will give the answer. We'll try to keep out of controversy for the present."[28]

In the meantime, Pope Pius XII had delivered, in early September, an address on church-state relations. He referred specifically in the talk to the American arrangement as an example "of the way in which the Church succeeds in flourishing in the most disparate situations."[29] Fenton published an English translation of the address in the November 1955 *American Ecclesiastical Review*, along with an article offering his own commentary on it. In his article, Fenton said the address makes clear that the pope's latest teaching on church and state "must clearly be normative for all future teaching and writing on Church-state relations by Catholics."[30]

"Everything Will Come Unstuck"

Murray maintained his silence. Over the following few years, he taught and lectured on topics like Christian education, public morality, media censorship, and the role of Catholicism in a pluralistic society. He became actively involved with the National Conference of Christians and Jews (well-known at the time for its highly successful residential youth leadership institutes) and also with the anticommunist and antisecularist Foundation for Religious Action in the Social and Civil Order. He was named as a consultor to President Eisenhower's Atomic Energy Commission and in September 1956 preached at Boston's annual Red Mass.[31]

---

[28] Ibid., 53.

[29] Pius XII, "The Holy Father's Address to the Tenth International Congress of Historical Sciences," AER 133 (November 1955): 340–51, at 347.

[30] Joseph Clifford Fenton, "The Holy Father's Statement on Relations between the Church and State," AER 133 (November 1955): 323–31, at 323.

[31] Pelotte, *John Courtney Murray*, 54–56.

In July 1958, a fellow Jesuit working at Georgetown University approached Murray to ask him to review an article he had written on Murray's work. Though helpful about the content, Murray was insistent that the Holy Office's demand that his work not be published applied by extension to its publication through the work of others. "I am sorry that you are thus stuck," he wrote, "after all the work you did. But I feel it necessary to let you know that you are stuck! Everything will come unstuck one fine day—but not yet. . . . It is too bad it has to end in some frustration, but in that you at least have company—my company!"[32]

Murray's frustration made him impatient for that "fine day" when things would "come unstuck." That same month, he wrote to McCormick saying he wanted to write an article that he hoped could be published in *Civiltà Cattolica* after receiving the personal approval of the pope himself. This, he thought, would be an effective way of clarifying the entire difficult matter.[33]

McCormick responded quickly:

> I am afraid you do not know the Rome of today. I very seriously doubt that there would be any chance of the Civiltà accepting an article by you on the subject of Church-State relations. No; we must be patient. . . . In the end what is correct in your stand will be justified. Meanwhile be content to stay on the sidelines, unless the hierarchy forces you into play: deepen and clarify your own position, and be ready with your solution approved, when the opportune time comes. That is not coming in the present Roman atmosphere.[34]

If by "the Roman atmosphere" McCormick meant Cardinal Ottaviani, he was right. Fenton commented in his personal diary in the fall of 1957 and again in the fall of 1958 (both times during visits to Rome that included frequent meetings with the cardinal) that Ottaviani was "still smarting" and "bitter" about "the attack the boy made on him

[32] Ibid., 58.
[33] Ibid., 58–59.
[34] Ibid., 59.

at the University." In the 1957 entry, Fenton noted, "If uncle lives the boy is definitely in trouble."[35]

Indeed, at that very time, Ottaviani's Holy Office was preparing a document that reaffirmed the classic thesis-synthesis doctrine on church and state and condemned a list of twenty-one propositions as unorthodox. Of those ideas listed, fourteen of them seem to have been drawn from Murray's 1950 memorandum to Montini.[36]

But that project was one of many suddenly held in suspension when, on the early morning of October 9, 1958, Pope Pius XII, after several years of poor health, died in his bed at Castel Gandolfo.

[35] Fenton journal, "My Tenth Trip to Rome, also the Eleventh, Twelfth, and Thirteenth Trips, August 1955–September 1958," box 1, folder 4, available at http://doc.wrlc.org/handle/2041/112121, November 13, 1957 and August 19, 1958.

[36] Komonchak, "The Crisis in Church-State Relationships in the U.S.A.," 685–86.

Chapter 11

The Truths We Hold
(1959–1960)

Though the richest, most significant, and most consequential theological work of John Courtney Murray's life is almost certainly the material he produced on religious freedom, it is not that for which he is most widely known. To most people familiar with American Catholicism in the twentieth century, he is known primarily as the author of *We Hold These Truths: Catholic Reflections on the American Proposition.*

Published in the fall of 1960, the book was a phenomenon in the world of Catholic and even secular publishing and earned him a place on the cover of *Time* magazine. And yet the book was not his idea, it included no original content, and—in comparison with the work on religious freedom that both preceded and followed it—it involved comparatively little effort on his part.

Origins

In 1957, Philip Scharper was the brand new editor-in-chief at the renowned Catholic publishing house Sheed & Ward. Scharper was a former Jesuit seminarian who had come to know Murray while studying at Woodstock Theological Seminary. Since then, he had taught theology for a short time at Fordham in New York and Xavier University in Cincinnati, and then worked as associate editor for two years at the prominent lay Catholic journal, *Commonweal.* In 1957, he had a long and distinguished career in Catholic publishing ahead of him, first at Sheed & Ward (where, in addition to his work with Murray, he would make available to the English-speaking world the likes of Karl Rahner, Hans Küng, and Edward Schillebeeckx), and then, starting in 1970, as cofounder of Orbis Books (where he introduced North American readers to Gustavo Guttierez, Leondardo Boff, Jon Sobrino, and other leading lights in the rich landscape of Latin American theology).[1]

Knowing Murray's sharp intellect and respecting him personally, Scharper approached Murray with an invitation to write a book on what it meant to evaluate the moral qualities of films in an authentically Christian way. Interested in the topic but busy with other projects and commitments, Murray graciously declined. The following year, Scharper approached Murray again, this time with an idea for a book on "the making of the Catholic mind." Again, Murray declined.[2]

By the spring of 1959, Scharper and his boss Frank Sheed were still keen to publish Murray but afraid that it would be a long time before he found the time to produce a monograph.[3] Probably they also had begun to sense a new moment in the church for work like Murray's, following the October 1958 election of John XXIII and January 1959 announcement of his intention to call the Second Vatican Council.

Sheed met with Murray and asked him to consider a collection of previously published articles on the general topic of American plural-ism. This time, Murray was receptive. But Scharper still had nothing from Murray at the end of year, so he took the liberty of preparing a rough outline for what he had in mind—a list of key Murray articles published in various journals between 1950 and 1958—and offered it to Murray. He also proposed a title: *The American Experiment and Catholic Experience.*[4]

Over the following months, Murray made some revisions to the articles, and the manuscript was assembled by July 1960. *We Hold*

---

[1] Stephen Bede Scharper, "Philip J. Scharper and the Editorial Vocation: Publishing Ideas of Consequence," *American Catholic Historian* 21, no. 3 (Summer 2003): 19–35, at 22–23; Glenn Fowler, "Philip Scharper, A Publisher, Dies," *New York Times*, May 8, 1985, available at http://www.nytimes.com/1985/05/08/nyregion/philip-scharper-a-publisher-dies.html.

[2] John F. Quinn, "The Enduring Influence of *We Hold These Truths*," *The Catholic Social Science Review* 16 (2011): 73–84, at 74.

[3] Scharper, "Philip J. Scharper and the Editorial Vocation," 26.

[4] Quinn, "The Enduring Influence of *We Hold These Truths*," 74.

These Truths was published in the fall, with an initial print run of fourteen thousand copies.[5]

The Truths We Hold

What resulted was a book on various aspects of the question of morality and religion in public life. Under this heading comes a wide range of topics, from education to nuclear war to laws prohibiting the sale of birth control. At its heart, though, *We Hold These Truths* offers a strong defense of the classical natural law tradition, presenting it as the necessary foundation of civil society in the United States. "Only the theory of natural law," Murray wrote, "can give an account of the public moral experience that is the public consensus."[6] The book is, in short, a work of political philosophy.[7]

The book paints Catholicism as the great source and custodian of the natural law tradition, while Protestantism only allows for its erosion. As Murray presented it, the American founding and its political tradition had strong roots in medieval Christianity. The result was a close compatibility between Catholicism and American democracy, including its particular arrangement of church and state. Murray had little to say in *We Hold These Truths* about the tensions between the two systems or the place of the Enlightenment in the American founding. "The American thesis," he writes in the second chapter, "is that government is not juridically omnipotent. Its powers are limited, and one of the principles of limitation is the distinction between state and church, in their purposes, methods, and manner of organization."[8]

At a time when ghetto Catholicism was still the norm, Murray made the case that it was precisely the thinking preserved by the

[5] Ibid., 74–75.

[6] John Courtney Murray, *We Hold These Truths: Catholic Reflections on the American Proposition* (New York: Sheed & Ward, 1960), 109.

[7] See, for example, Robert F. Cuervo, "John Courtney Murray and the Public Philosophy," and Peter Augustine Lawler, "Murray's Natural Law Articulation of the American Proposition," in *John Courtney Murray and the American Civil Conversation*, ed. Robert P. Hunt and Kenneth L. Grasso (Grand Rapids, MI: Eerdmans, 1992), 67–88 and 116–34, respectively.

[8] Murray, *We Hold These Truths*, 68.

Catholic tradition that made America great from the start and that could preserve America's greatness in the present day, when the dangerous philosophical and cultural currents of secularism threatened its future.

"Always Stimulating and Sometimes Brilliant"

Somewhat surprisingly to all, *We Hold These Truths* quickly became a best seller for Sheed & Ward, and within a few months, it had been cited approvingly by a US Supreme Court justice in a case related to film censorship.[9]

The *New York Times* published a review of the book on October 30, 1960. Catholic journalist John Cogley (a former executive editor of *Commonweal*) wrote that the book was "probably the most significant Roman Catholic statement on American democracy ever published." Its "thirteen always stimulating and sometimes brilliant chapters," he said, resulted in "a unified work, grandly conceived, consistently argued and integrally styled." Calling Murray "as Catholic as Aquinas, as Jesuit as Loyola, and as American as the authors of the Federalist Papers," Cogley said *We Hold These Truths* "represents a major conservative statement on the meaning of America." He did criticize it as sometimes "lacking in a sense of the real, or at least the realistic."[10]

Joseph Fenton, of course, took a different view. Though silent about the book until a year after its publication, he then commented in his *American Ecclesiastical Review*, returning to ground he'd covered before. Acknowledging that the book was "very well written," he said that Murray's thinking "bears not the slightest resemblance" to Catholic teaching on church-state issues. He warned against teachers of doctrine who, by their "sympathy for the liberalism of the day," obscured the truth that every man and every society is objectively

---

[9] Quinn, "The Enduring Influence of *We Hold These Truths*," 78.

[10] John Cogley, "Catholic Tradition and American Present," *New York Times*, October 30, 1960, http://select.nytimes.com/gst/abstract.html?res=F00610FC3 B541A7A93C2AA178BD95F448685F9.

bound to worship Christ in the Catholic liturgy.[11] A review in the *Homiletic and Pastoral Review* was also critical.[12]

In secular publications, political conservatives were more enthusiastic. William Buckley wrote in the *National Review* that the book "leaves the reader stunned with admiration and pleasure." The conservative journal *Modern Age* said the book was "long overdue for those American conservatives who find themselves, nowadays, hard put to . . . say what it is in the American political system that they should be trying to conserve."[13]

In 1964, with Murray now much better known to the American public following the *Time* cover and his work at the Second Vatican Council, Doubleday released an Image paperback edition of the book.[14]

Kennedy's Houston Speech

In the fall of 1960, Murray played a brief and minor role in a very significant moment of the John F. Kennedy presidential campaign. Just over a decade after Paul Blanshard's best-selling *American Freedom and Catholic Power*, Kennedy's Catholic faith caused many Americans to question his fitness for the office. He chose to address the issue directly on the campaign trail, in a speech to a group of Protestant ministers called the Greater Houston Ministerial Association, on September 12, 1960. The speech was written by Kennedy campaign advisor Ted Sorenson (later special counsel to the president), who made ample

[11] Joseph Clifford Fenton, "Doctrine and Tactic in Catholic Pronouncements on Church and State," AER 145 (October 1961): 266–76, at 266, 271, 276.

[12] M. Joseph Costelloe "Father Murray's 'Reflections,'" *Homiletic and Pastoral Review* 61 (May 1961): 812, cited in Quinn, "The Enduring Influence of *We Hold These Truths*," 77–78.

[13] William F. Buckley, "Nihil Obstat," *National Review* 10 (January 28, 1961): 56–57; Willmoore Kendall, "Natural Law and 'Natural Right,'" *Modern Age* 6 (Winter 1961–1962): 94, 96. Both cited in Quinn, "The Enduring Influence of *We Hold These Truths*," 76–77.

[14] Quinn, "The Enduring Influence of *We Hold These Truths*," 73–84, at 73. Quinn notes that the book went out of print in the 1970s. A decade later, responding to a resurgence of interest in Murray's work among Catholic conservatives, Sheed & Ward published a new edition. After purchasing Sheed & Ward in 2002, Rowman & Littlefield republished *We Hold These Truths* in 2005.

reference in preparing it to Kennedy's own previous statements about religion. Sorenson later wrote that he contacted Murray and read the speech over the phone to him prior to the trip to Houston, "in the hopes of avoiding any loose wording . . . that would unnecessarily stir up the Catholic press."[15] Sorenson does not comment at all on Murray's reaction to or opinion of the speech. He suggests that a conversation with Bishop (later Cardinal) John Wright may have influenced its content as well.[16]

In the speech, Kennedy offered his political credo:

> I believe in an America that is officially neither Catholic, Protestant, nor Jewish; where no public official either requests or accepts instructions on public policy from the Pope, the National Council of Churches, or any other ecclesiastical source; where no religious body seeks to impose its will directly or indirectly upon the general populace or the public acts of its officials; and where religious liberty is so indivisible that an act against one church is treated as an act against all.

Insisting that "I do not speak for my church on public matters, and the church does not speak for me," Kennedy said that if the unlikely time ever came that carrying out his duties as president meant violating his conscience, he would resign the office, adding, "and I hope any conscientious public servant would do the same."[17]

Many credit the speech for effectively confronting the discomfort of many Americans at the idea of a Catholic president. It might reasonably be suggested that Murray's *We Hold These Truths*, published in October, and its prominent review in the *New York Times* that month, provided further aid in this regard, but perhaps not to a great degree, since it did not have the time to come to the attention of many readers before the November election.

Kennedy, of course, was elected president on November 8, 1960.

[15] Theodore Sorenson, *Kennedy* (New York: Harper & Row, 1965), 189–91.

[16] Ibid., 191.

[17] "Transcript: JFK's Speech on His Religion," at http://www.npr.org/templates/story/story.php?storyId=16920600.

On the Cover of *Time*

The December 12, 1960, issue of *Time* magazine featured Murray's face on the cover. At the time, *Time* was a media juggernaut, the most popular and highly regarded among American newsmagazines, reaching tens of millions of readers every week. (*"Time* practically defined what it meant to be mass media," one journalist wrote recently. "It was a brand for pretty much everybody."[18]) The cover appearance, in Murray's case, crowned him as a sort of celebrity intellectual of the day.

The image of Murray was a portrait painted by Boris Chaliapin, a prolific *Time* cover artist who created over four hundred cover images for the magazine between 1942 and 1970.[19] It depicted a stern-looking Murray in his clerical suit, against a backdrop that featured the title page of a text by Cardinal Robert Bellarmine (to be specific, Volume 1 of Bellarmine's seven-volume *Disputationes de Controversiis Christianae Fidei*), a key figure in Murray's telling of the history of the church's approach to religious freedom. Murray's name ran across the bottom of the image and a bright yellow band crossed the cover's top right corner reading, "U.S. CATHOLICS & THE STATE."

The long accompanying article, by *Time* religion writer Douglas Auchincloss, was largely a skillful presentation of the main ideas of *We Hold These Truths*. It also included reference to Murray's conflicts with Fenton and Connell in the *American Ecclesiastical Review* and noted briefly that that "scholarly drumfire of debate" had ended when Murray was ordered to submit all his writings for approval to Jesuit officials in Rome. There was no mention of the Vatican's formal condemnation of four doctrinal errors in his work, as these had not been made public.

"The [Catholic] church of 50 years ago," Auchincloss wrote,

[18] Joshua Macht, "Running Out of Time: The Slow, Sad Demise of a Great American Magazine," *The Atlantic*, April 5, 2013, http://www.theatlantic.com/business/archive/2013/04/running-out-of-time-the-slow-sad-demise-of-a-great-american-magazine/274713/.

[19] View the cover at http://content.time.com/time/covers/0,16641,19601212,00.html. The original hangs today in the offices of *America* magazine in New York City. On Chaliapin, see Harry J. Weil, "Catching up with Mr. Time," *ARTNews*, April 9, 2013, at http://www.artnews.com/2013/04/09/catching-up-with-time-mag-top-portraitist/.

was largely a church of immigrants, whose concern was to protect and build their minority religion in a Protestant land while showing their fellow Americans what all-out patriots they were. Today, an increasing number of well-educated and theologically sophisticated young Catholics are beginning to take part in what Father Murray calls "building the city"— contributing both to the civic machinery and the need for consensus beneath it.

The Rev. John Courtney Murray, SJ, is unquestionably the intellectual bellwether of this new Catholic and American frontier.[20]

---

[20] Douglas Auchincloss, "To Be Catholic and American," *Time*, December 12, 1960, http://content.time.com/time/subscriber/article/0,33009,871923,00.html.

Part Four

Vindication and Vatican II

Chapter 12

Disinvited . . . and Invited
(1959–1963)

Pope John XXIII described himself as "trembling a little with emotion but at the same time humbly resolute in my purpose" as he stood before a small group of cardinals gathered at Rome's Basilica of Saint Paul outside the Walls on January 25, 1959.[1] Less than one hundred days into his pontificate, he had decided to give voice to an idea that he would later attribute to "a flash of heavenly light" and "an inspiration from heaven."[2] He would summon an ecumenical council, he told them, a gathering of the world's bishops to deliberate authoritatively on matters important to the church's faith and life.

It did not take long for preparations for the council to kick into gear, first in Rome and soon after in diocesan chanceries around the world. Although—as we will see below—John Courtney Murray was notably absent from direct participation in the first important stages of the council, there is another sense in which he was a powerful presence in the process right from the start.

In a June 1959 letter, Vatican Secretary of State Cardinal Domenico Tardini invited every bishop in the world to submit his opinion about topics the council should address. Among the responses the Vatican

---

[1] Giuseppe Alberigo, "The Announcement of the Council: From the Security of the Fortress to the Lure of the Quest," in *History of Vatican II*, vol. 1, ed. Giuseppe Alberigo and Joseph A. Komonchak (Maryknoll, NY: Orbis Books, 1995), 1–54, at 1.

[2] The former in his opening address for the first session of the council, on October 11, 1962, the latter in an address to non-Catholic observers to the council two days later. See ibid., 7 and 6.

received from bishops in the United States, a great many of them—a full one-fourth, in fact—proposed religious freedom. The theological controversy that had been brewing throughout the decade in response to Murray's work surely played a role in their thinking. Indeed, several of the suggestions submitted to Rome from US bishops (including those of Cardinals Richard Cushing of Boston and John O'Hara of Philadelphia and Archbishops Karl Alter of Cincinnati and Paul Schulte of Indianapolis) clearly reflected Murray's influence on their approach to the issue. Only one—that of Newark archbishop Thomas Boland—reflected the thesis-hypothesis approach.[3] (As would be seen when the topic eventually was raised at the council, their near agreement on the value of Murray's approach was decidedly not shared by many of their brother bishops around the world, especially those who worked at the Vatican.)

Disinvited

But that influence was as close as Murray would get to Vatican II for some time. Indeed, it looked for a while like he would not be involved at all, while Joseph Fenton was summoned quickly and directly to the center of the action. Fenton was invited by Cardinal Ottaviani to serve as his theological expert, or *peritus*, during the preparatory stages of the council and then again during every stage of conciliar work that followed. As the council opened, many of Murray's peers in the theological academy—including several who had, like him, previously labored under similar Roman suspicion or censure—were also called to be *periti* (the plural of *peritus*) for various bishops of the world. Murray, however, was not.

Whether this is because he was excluded from the start from consideration or, somewhat more dramatically, was initially invited only to be subsequently "disinvited" from serving as *peritus*, is unclear. Murray himself spoke of his being "disinvited," but there is, so far as I can determine, no archival evidence that he received a formal invitation that was later rescinded (while the record of his eventual invitation is

---

[3] Joseph A. Komonchak, "The American Contribution to *Dignitatis Humanae*: The Role of John Courtney Murray, SJ," *U.S. Catholic Historian* 24, no. 1 (Winter 2006): 5.

easy to find). Could it have been only a colorful way of speaking of his exclusion?

Murray's reference to the situation comes in a letter to a fellow Jesuit, written in February 1967, five years after the fact: "It was not Ottaviani who 'disinvited' me to the first session; it was the Apostolic Delegate [to the United States, Archbishop Egidio Vagnozzi] (and I know this only on confidential information)."[4] But even this suggests he might have been excluded rather than invited then disinvited, since the rescission of a formal invitation surely would not have come anonymously or confidentially. Perhaps Murray had heard through informal channels that he had been considered for the invitation, but that the idea was nixed in advance by Vagnozzi.

Michael Novak, a journalist at the council, wrote in 1964 (still a couple of years after the fact) that Murray had been invited to attend the first session of the council, but "the invitation was suddenly and embarrassingly withdrawn."[5] Following Murray's death in 1967, writer John Cogley wrote in *America* magazine of a dinner he had with Murray while the first session of the council was going on,

> the session from which, as he put it, he had been abruptly un-invited. "Do you feel bad about it?" I asked. "I do," he said. "A man doesn't live long, and if something big is going on, a man feels that he ought to be there." The statement was as impersonally worded as a proposition from *We Hold These Truths*. There was no note of having been abused in it, no self-pity, no plea for sympathy—simply the unadorned expression of how a "man" under certain circumstances truly feels.[6]

---

[4] Donald E. Pelotte, *John Courtney Murray: Theologian in Conflict* (New York: Paulist Press, 1975), 77n28. The letter is to Richard Regan. Note that Murray's nephew recalled, decades later, Murray being quite specific about the matter: "I was invited, and then I was disinvited. The distinction is crucial" (Mark Williams, "Memories of 'Uncle Jack': A Nephew Remembers John Courtney Murray," in *Finding God in All Things: Celebrating Bernard Lonergan, John Courtney Murray, and Karl Rahner*, ed. Mark Bosco and David Stagaman [New York: Fordham University Press, 2007], 92–98, at 97).

[5] Michael Novak, *The Open Church* (New York: Macmillian, 1964), 257.

[6] Quoted in Pelotte, *John Courtney Murray*, 108n28.

Whether by exclusion or disinvitation, Murray was back at Woodstock, still forbidden to publish on the topic of religious freedom, while Joseph Fenton played an important role from the start. Fenton, ever the warrior, must surely have seen the moment as a vindication, a demonstration of who, in his theological battle with Murray, was on the side of the angels. Indeed, in his journal of November–December 1960, while working in Rome preparing for the council, he transcribed for himself yet again the four doctrinal errors formally ascribed to Murray's work by the Holy Office six years earlier, and then wrote that "it seems quite imperative to me that the teaching embodying the contradictions of these four condemned propositions be submitted to the forthcoming Council and set forth by the Council itself."[7]

He was also quite confident of the sort of outcome the council would have. Responding to a June 1961 *Our Sunday Visitor* article that suggested the council might prove to be a revolutionary moment in the history of the church, Fenton wrote in *AER* that there would certainly be no "softening of Catholic teaching or directives with reference to religious societies and religious doctrines other than the Catholic." He wrote, "Doctrinally, then, there will be no revolution in Catholic attitudes. There will be no readjustment of Catholic ideas. . . . [The words *dialogue* and *pluralism*] in every probability . . . will be dead and forgotten in a very few years."[8]

First Steps

Religious freedom was included from the start in conciliar preparatory work. On December 27, 1960, a commission of the brand new Secretariat for Christian Unity (SCU) met for the first time in Fribourg, Switzerland, to prepare a draft document on the topic. Pope John had created the SCU earlier that year in such a way that it had no counterparts or parallels in the Roman Curia. Council historian Massimo

---

[7] Fenton journal, "Notes of My Previous Fourteenth Trip to Rome Continued from the Previous Volume 11/18/1960, November 18, 1960–December 12, 1960," folder 1, box 6, available at http://doc.wrlc.org/handle/2041/112123, November 18, 1960.

[8] Joseph Clifford Fenton, "Revolutions in Catholic Attitudes," *AER* 145 (August 1961): 120–29, at 122–23.

Faggioli calls the establishment of the SCU "the most important and creative decision of John XXIII for the whole development of Vatican II."[9] The pope entrusted its leadership to Cardinal Augustin Bea, a Jesuit who was best known until then as a gifted Scripture scholar.

Bea had not initially intended that the SCU would prepare texts for consideration at the council but set to work in the task, "with the apparent encouragement of the Pope," after it became clear that the important preparatory Theological Commission headed by Cardinal Ottaviani intended to ignore questions related to ecumenism.[10] The SCU officials saw religious freedom as an ecumenical issue mainly because so many non-Catholics distrusted the church on account of the traditional thesis-hypothesis teaching. Without addressing this, their thinking went, ecumenism would be nearly impossible.[11]

Protestant leaders seemed to agree. Between October 1960 and September 1961, for example, the periodical of the World Council of Churches, *The Ecumenical Review*, published twelve articles—a full quarter of all articles published during that time—on the topic.[12] The Presbyterian theologian Robert McAfee Brown, who served as an ecumenical observer at the council, said in a speech to the bishops of Canada, "I do not think there is a single direct thing that the Council can do that will have more immediate effect in bettering Catholic-Protestant relations than a forthright and unambiguous statement favoring full religious liberty for all. The reason a statement on religious liberty is so important, therefore, is because (to put it bluntly for the sake of time and not pause over ecumenical niceties) the Catholic Church is not trusted on this point."[13]

---

[9] Massimo Faggioli, *John XXIII: The Medicine of Mercy* (Collegeville, MN: Liturgical Press, 2014), 116.

[10] Joseph A. Komonchak, "The Struggle for the Council during the Preparation of Vatican II," in *History of Vatican II*, vol. 1, ed. Giuseppe Alberigo and Joseph A. Komonchak (Maryknoll, NY: Orbis Books, 1995), 167–356, at 265–66.

[11] See, for example, the comments of Bishop Emile-Joseph De Smedt to the council on November 19, 1963, in Richard J. Regan, *Conflict and Consensus: Religious Freedom and the Second Vatican Council* (New York: Macmillan, 1967), 38.

[12] John Coleman "The Achievement of Religious Freedom," *U.S. Catholic Historian* 24, no. 1 (Winter 2006): 21–32, at 24.

[13] Ibid.

At its December 1960 meeting, the SCU commission began working from a paper prepared by Bishop Emile-Joseph De Smedt of Bruges, Belgium, as basis for discussion.[14] (De Smedt, then fifty-one, would lead the SCU's efforts on behalf of religious liberty right up to the close of the council five years later.) The SCU developed their draft text and formally submitted it to the Conciliar Preparatory Commission (CPC) for consideration on June 18, 1962. Though the SCU was not an official preconciliar commission—and therefore not officially sanctioned to submit such texts directly—Pope John had instructed Bea to send the document to the CPC "without any other commission intervening."[15] The text avoided the thesis-hypothesis approach to religious freedom, rejected the idea that the state has an obligation to worship God, and offered the church's approval of laws that protected the religious freedom of all.[16]

At the same time the SCU was developing its text, the TC—headed by Ottaviani—produced, among several others, a schema on the church that included a chapter on "Relations between Church and State and Religious Tolerance." Even here, John Courtney Murray's presence is strong, since this TC document was prepared primarily by Fr. Rosaire Gagnebet, the Dominican theologian who had penned, two years earlier, the document under preparation for the Holy Office condemning contemporary errors on the topic of religious freedom (largely those Murray had been advocating). The TC's preconciliar schema on the church basically reproduced Gagnebet's earlier document as the chapter on church and state, with minimal changes. Throughout the TC's revision process on their draft, the chapter remained very similar to the original anti-Murray draft document and amounted to a restatement of the classical approach that Murray had been criticizing.[17] The TC submitted this text to the CPC on June 18, 1962.

[14] Regan, *Conflict and Consensus*, 13. Komonchak says it was "prepared by [theologian] L[ouis] Janssen and presented by Bishop de Smedt" ("The Struggle for the Council during the Preparation of Vatican II," 298).

[15] Komonchak, "The Struggle for the Council during the Preparation of Vatican II," 298, n467.

[16] Ibid., 298–99; Regan, *Conflict and Consensus*, 13–20.

[17] Komonchak, "The Struggle for the Council during the Preparation of Vatican II," 296–97; Regan, *Conflict and Consensus*, 20, 24.

And so at the same meeting, the CPC received two documents—one from the SCU, one from the TC—that approached the same question with dramatically different stances. At that meeting, Cardinal Ottaviani briefly introduced his own group's text and then launched into a harsh criticism of the SCU text, saying it clearly was influenced by non-Catholic thinking and insisting that the SCU lacked the competence to propose a conciliar text in the first place. Only his text, he said, should be considered.

Bea responded with strong objections, insisting his office did have the competence to submit the text and pointing out that Ottaviani's theological commission had refused to collaborate with him throughout the course of its drafting. A long discussion, which one historian of the council called "the most dramatic confrontation witnessed by that body," ensued. Ultimately, it was decided that the pope would have to resolve the matter.[18]

Presented with the conflict, Pope John created an ad hoc commission representing both offices and instructed them to reconcile their conflicting texts. Though the SCU revised its text in an effort to include perspectives from the TC text, the ad hoc commission never actually met and no real progress was made.

In August, as the opening of the council approached, Baltimore's Archbishop Lawrence Sheehan shared the TC draft on the church with Murray for his feedback. In his response to Sheehan, Murray referred to the classical theory supported in the document by Ottaviani and his collaborators:

> Few seem to realize how dreadfully weak their position is—if it were exposed to free and full discussion. Presently it maintains itself only by the power of the Holy Office to shut up anyone who presumes to question it. . . . We have a heaven-sent opportunity to effect a genuine development of doctrine in this matter—an absolutely necessary development and one that can quite readily be effected. The opportunity should not be missed.[19]

[18] Komonchak, "The Struggle for the Council during the Preparation of Vatican II," 299; cf. Regan, *Conflict and Consensus*, 26.

[19] Pelotte, *John Courtney Murray*, 79–80.

That same month, the bishops of the United States assembled for their annual meeting and produced a joint pastoral letter about the council that was about to begin. From the perspective of history, it seems remarkably prescient. They expressed their conviction that they had a special contribution to make to this historic event. Despite being a much younger community that lacked the long tradition of other peoples of the globe, American Catholicism could offer to the council the advantages "which have come to the Church from living and growing in an atmosphere of religious and political freedom."[20]

The First Session Opens

With around 2,500 bishops gathered at the Vatican from around the world, Pope John formally opened the council on October 11, 1962. The address he offered to the council fathers that day, which he wrote himself,[21] remains one of the best known of his pontificate. Faggioli calls it "one of the most consequential speeches in church history," for it "changed the horizon of expectations from the council" among those who participated in it.[22]

John's speech was a bold and inspiring vision of a council that had Christ, "ever resplendent as the center of history and life," as its center. In a passage for which the address would become most remembered, John decisively rejected any defensiveness and isolationism of the church toward the world. He said he regretted having to listen at times to "the complaints of people who, though burning with zeal, are not endowed with an overabundance of discretion or measure. They see in modern times nothing but prevarication and ruin." Rejecting the idea that the present was worse than the past, he dismissed "these prophets of doom, who are always forecasting disaster."[23]

---

[20] Klaus Wittstadt, "On the Eve of the Second Vatican Council (July 1–October 10, 1962)," in *History of Vatican II*, vol. 1, ed. Giuseppe Alberigo and Joseph A. Komonchak (Maryknoll, NY: Orbis Books, 1995), 405–500, at 408–9.

[21] Andrea Riccardi, "The Tumultuous Opening Days of the Council," in *History of Vatican II*, vol. 2, ed. Giuseppe Alberigo and Joseph A. Komonchak (Maryknoll, NY: Orbis: 1997), 1–67, at 15n29.

[22] Faggioli, *John XXIII*, 124.

[23] Cited in Riccardi, "The Tumultuous Opening Days of the Council," 15.

Two days after John's memorable speech, Joseph Fenton was troubled. He confided to his journal, "I had always thought this council was dangerous. It was started for no sufficient reason. There was too much talk about what it was supposed to accomplish. Now I am afraid that real trouble is on the way." He wrote a few days later of being "shocked by the bad theology" in material proposed for conciliar discussion on the liturgy and frustrated that there was only one "intelligent and faithful" member of the Secretariat for Christian Unity (which would later be responsible for the document on religious liberty). He lamented, "We should, I believe, face the facts. Since the death of St. Pius X the Church has been directed by weak and liberal popes, who have flooded the hierarchy with unworthy and stupid men. This present conciliar set-up makes this all the more apparent. . . . From surface appearances it would seem that the Lord Christ is abandoning His Church."[24]

The council took up the topic of liturgy first of all on its agenda that first session. It made some progress on a few other subjects as well, but religious freedom was not one of them. One early decision, though, would ultimately have a significant impact on the fate of Murray's work. On October 19, Pope John raised SCU to equal rank with the other conciliar commissions. That meant it formally had the authority to develop schemata and present them to the council fathers.

Invited to the Council (and Banned from Catholic University)

It became clear during the first session, both to the world's bishops and to the general public, that many of the *periti* were playing a major role in the council's work. Some of the highest regarded among them—Henri de Lubac, Yves Congar, Joseph Ratzinger, and Karl Rahner, for example—were a group of young guns, a few of whom had been suspected by the Holy Office just a few years earlier of heretical teaching. These same men were now influencing the interventions delivered by the bishops on the council floor in significant ways. They presented public lectures in Rome that were well attended by bishops

---

[24] Fenton journal, "Journal of My Sixteenth, Seventeenth, Eighteenth, and Nineteenth Trips to Rome, March 1962–February 1963," box 1, folder 9, available at http://doc.wrlc.org/handle/2041/112136, October 13 and 19, 1962.

and laity alike, and they were quoted often by the worldwide media in its council coverage.

Though sixty-one American priests had served as *periti* during the first session, it was clear to many of the bishops that one man ought to have been among them. On February 11, 1963—about two months after the close of the first session—Cardinal Francis Spellman, the archbishop of New York, wrote to Vatican Secretary of State Cardinal Amleto Cicognani that

> a number of Bishops and theologians have spoken to me about the fact that [Murray] has not been named among the "periti" for the Ecumenical Council. The number of persons making inquiry has notably increased during the period since the close of the first session of the Council. I know Your Eminence is acquainted with Father Murray, and unless there is some reason to the contrary of which I am unaware, I would strongly recommend that Father Murray be included among the number of those designated as "periti."[25]

Ironically, in the very same week that the most powerful Catholic prelate in America was writing to Rome to insist that Murray be named a Council *peritus*, The Catholic University of America was announcing that Murray was banned from speaking on the campus. In mid-February, CUA acknowledged that Murray's name—along with those of American Jesuit Gustave Weigel, American Benedictine Godfrey Diekmann, and German Hans Küng, all highly regarded theologians—had been rejected from a list of twelve that the Graduate Student Council had considered inviting for a lecture series. The news received national attention[26] and provoked much discussion about academic freedom. Perhaps most notable were the objections voiced publicly by Baltimore's Cardinal Lawrence Sheehan, St. Louis's Cardinal Joseph Ritter, Atlanta's Archbishop Paul Hallinan, and Cincinnati's

---

[25] Spellman to Cicognani, February 11, 1963, Archives of the Archdiocese of New York, St. Joseph's Seminary, Dunwoodie, Cardinal Spellman—Literary Works, Vatican Council II Correspondence, S/C-110, folder 1.

[26] See, for example, "Religion: Silencing the Outspoken," *Time*, February 22, 1963, http://content.time.com/time/subscriber/article/0,33009,828041,00.html.

Archbishop Karl Alter, each members of the CUA board of directors. Acknowledging the university's right to ban speakers from its campus, Sheehan called for "an investigation of the forces responsible for suspicion and fear," and explicitly mentioned the *American Ecclesiastical Review* as one of them.[27]

Nevertheless, Cicognani's office notified Spellman several weeks later that Murray had been named a *peritus*. Spellman mailed the official notification to Murray on April 9, saying he was "very happy" to send it and offering his "sincere congratulations."[28]

The official document from Cicognani notes, in Latin, that the council would address questions of "freedom and religious tolerance, which are not without debated controversy" in its upcoming session. It reminded Murray that it was not the council's intent to answer questions that it would be premature and hazardous to approach in a definitive way and mentions the two schemas in development, SCU's on religious freedom and TC's on religious tolerance. "Because of the pastoral purpose of the council and because of the expectations of many," the document concludes, "this question must be considered carefully."[29]

Pope John's *Pacem in Terris*

On April 11, 1963, perhaps the very day Murray was receiving his letter from Spellman with his official council accreditation enclosed, Pope John XXIII promulgated a new encyclical letter, *Pacem in Terris* ("Peace on Earth"). Written in the wake of the terror of the Cuban Missile Crisis, which Pope John had a hand in bringing to a peaceful resolution the previous October, the encyclical was a stirring defense of human rights. Among the many human rights defended by the pope, the encyclical included "that of being able to worship God in

---

[27] C. Joseph Nuesse, *The Catholic University of America: A Centennial History* (Washington, DC: The Catholic University of America Press, 1990), 395. See also Pelotte, *John Courtney Murray*, 81, and Novak, *The Open Church*, 15.

[28] Spellman to Murray, April 9, 1963, New York archdiocesan archives.

[29] "Animadversiones de Schematibus Reformandis a Commissionibus Propriis Secundum Propositiones Commissiones de Concilii Laboribus Coordinandis," NY Archd Archives. My translation from the Latin.

accordance with the right dictates of his own conscience, and to profess his religion both in private and in public."[30]

"In one sentence of one encyclical," wrote Richard Regan, SJ, "John appeared to work a veritable Copernican revolution in the theology of religious freedom." Still, he noted, the sentence perhaps raised more questions than it answered and left plenty of room for interpretation to those disinclined to acknowledge such a right. What makes the dictates of one's conscience "right," for example? And how far does the right to profess one's religion in public extend? Do people who do not believe in God have rights to express their thinking too?[31]

Indeed, though Fenton chose not to comment on the encyclical in *AER*, Francis Connell explained in its pages that the Latin of the official text allowed for more than one interpretation of the meaning of Pope John's sentence on religious freedom. "Evidently," Connell wrote, "Pope John XXIII intended to leave unanswered the question whether a person has a real right to embrace in good faith a false religion, or has a real right to accept only the religion that is objectively true."[32]

Pope John, who had been told he was dying of stomach cancer, knew when he signed *Pacem in Terris* that it would serve as his parting words to the world. He died on June 3, 1963, less than four months before the opening of the council's second session.

---

[30] John XXIII, encyclical letter *Pacem in Terris*, 14, available at http://www.vatican.va/holy_father/john_xxiii/encyclicals/documents/hf_j-xxiii_enc_11041963_pacem_en.html.

[31] Regan, *Conflict and Consensus*, 9.

[32] Francis J. Connell, "Freedom of Worship," *AER* 149 (September 1963): 201–2, at 202.

Chapter 13

Peritus Quidam

(1963–1964)

W hen the new pope, Paul VI, opened the second session of
the council on September 29, 1963, the status of the SCU's
religious freedom schema was quite unclear. Reading accounts of the conciliar work during the months leading up to that opening[1] leaves one with images of children squabbling on a playground,
refusing to share toys with one another.

"A Glorious Victory for the Good Guys"

At a plenary meeting of the SCU the previous February, a new
draft had been developed. Surely feeling far less beholden now to the
TC, thanks to its newly independent status as a conciliar commission,
Bea's group had thrown out the compromise draft it had developed
following the conflict over the two texts on state and church. This time,
SCU chose mostly to avoid directly addressing the topic of state and
church, sticking specifically to religious freedom. By the time Murray
came on board as a *peritus*, the writing of this new draft had already
been completed, and Murray was tasked with preparing its footnotes.[2]

---

[1] E.g., Claude Soetens, "The Ecumenical Commitment of the Catholic Church," in
History of Vatican II, vol. 3, ed. Giuseppe Alberigo and Joseph A. Komonchak (Maryknoll, NY: Orbis Books, 2000), 257–345, at 279–80; and Richard Regan, *Conflict and
Consensus: Religious Freedom and the Second Vatican Council* (New York: Macmillan,
1967), 33–36.

[2] Soetens, "The Ecumenical Commitment of the Catholic Church," in Alberigo
and Komonchak, 278.

Ottaviani's TC—which needed to approve the schema before it could be printed and distributed to the council fathers—did not reject the text; it simply did nothing, no matter how many times it was prompted to address it.[3] This delaying strategy could only benefit the cause of opposition to the schema, since every passing day decreased the chances of the document ever being addressed.

One must recall that it was by no means clear yet that the council would convene for a total of four sessions or even that it would produce much of any lasting significance. The previous autumn, Boston's Cardinal Cushing had been so convinced the council was not worth his time that he had returned home to the United States only three weeks into the first session (that is, less than halfway through it), saying publicly that he left because his poor Latin skills left him unable to understand the council's deliberations well enough.[4] When the prominent Italian Cardinal Giuseppe Siri was asked in a March 1963 *America* magazine interview what he most wished to see happen at the upcoming second session, the first words out of his mouth were "I very much wish to see the Council come to the completion of its work." He went on to wonder aloud why there should be any need for the council to address any social questions, since "it is so thoroughly treated in the encyclicals of the Popes. . . . It's all there."[5]

In the fall, at the request of the US bishops, Murray prepared a four-page memo listing several reasons that including religious freedom on the conciliar agenda was an "urgent" matter. "It would be a cause of wonderment," the memo concluded, "not to say scandal, if the Council were to fail to speak to the question or speak to it in obscure or ambiguous terms."[6]

[3] Xavier Rynne, *The Second Session: The Debates and Decrees of Vatican Council II, September 29 to December 4, 1963* (New York: Farrar, Straus, & Co., 1964), 39 and 191.

[4] Walter M. Abbott, "Cardinal Cushing," *America* 108 (June 15, 1963): 864–67, at 864.

[5] Walter M. Abbott, "Truth First and Always," *America* 108 (March 30, 1963): 434–46, at 435.

[6] Joseph A. Komonchak, "The American Contribution to *Dignitatis Humanae*: The Role of John Courtney Murray," *U.S. Catholic Historian* 24, no. 1 (Winter 2006): 1–20, at 7.

During a meeting of their full body in Rome, the American bishops adopted Murray's memo as the basis of a formal petition from them that the schema be restored to the council's agenda. On behalf of their entire body and with a cover letter from himself, Cardinal Spellman sent the petition on October 22 to Cardinal Cicognani (previously apostolic delegate to the United States, he was now the Vatican secretary of state) and to the council presidents and moderators. Spellman also personally brought a copy to the pope.[7]

At the beginning of November, Pope Paul intervened. Making explicit reference to the US bishops' petition, he insisted to Ottaviani that the TC begin meeting more frequently and that it quickly address the SCU draft on religious freedom.[8]

Though he obviously preferred not to do it, Ottaviani therefore convened a meeting of the TC on November 11 and 12. Included in the room were at least four cardinals (Ottaviani, Browne, Franic, Leger), several archbishops and bishops, and also several *periti*. Murray was there, as was Joseph Fenton, Bernard Häring, Karl Rahner, and Rosaire Gagnebet.

Cardinals Ottaviani and Browne and Archbishop Parente—all of whom would oppose the idea of religious freedom throughout the entire course of the council—each spoke against the SCU schema. Bishop Charue of Namur spoke strongly in its favor and then suggested that the *periti* present speak on the issue. When Murray was called on to speak, Ottaviani, who was nearly blind, did not recognize him. He quietly asked Cardinal Leger, seated beside him, who he was. Leger replied tactfully, *"Peritus quidam"* ("One of the periti").[9] Häring and Rahner also spoke in favor of the text at the meeting.

The next day, prior to the reconvening of the full body of the TC, a subcommittee led by Leger voted unanimously that the schema be

---

[7] Donald E. Pelotte, *John Courtney Murray: Theologian in Conflict* (New York: Paulist Press, 1975), 82; Komonchak, "The American Contribution to *Dignitatis Humanae*," 8.

[8] Richard J. Regan, *Conflict and Consensus: Religious Freedom and the Second Vatican Council* (New York: Macmillan, 1967), 35; Soetens, "The Ecumenical Commitment of the Catholic Church," 280.

[9] Donald R. Campion and Daniel J. O'Hanlon, "Council Jottings," *America* 109 (November 30, 1963): 701–2, at 701.

included in debate on the council floor. When the full group gathered, Ottaviani again tried to delay, but the members of the TC voted eighteen to five to release the schema for discussion.[10] In a letter to the rector back at Woodstock, Murray described the tense meeting and called the conclusion "a glorious victory for the Good Guys."[11] There is no question that without the pressure from the US bishops, supported by Murray's work, the SCU schema on religious freedom might never have gone as far as this in the face of opposition and stalling from the powerful Ottaviani.

"With Force and with Fire"

Finally, on November 19, 1963—exactly two months after the second session had opened and fifteen days before it was scheduled to wrap up—the council fathers got their first look at the text on religious freedom (I will call this Text 1). By this time, it had been decided by the SCU that this schema was to be considered as chapter 5 of the document on ecumenism that the council was considering.

The document approached religious freedom primarily by way of "freedom of conscience." The theme of conscience was prominent in the text, and the terms "religious freedom" and "freedom of conscience" were used almost interchangeably.[12] Since faith must always be a free act, the text argued, Catholics "are to respect and esteem the right of duty of non-Catholics to follow the dictates of their own conscience, even when, after serious and adequate investigation, it errs in good faith." It demanded that all governments allow all their citizens to follow the dictates of their conscience in religious matters.[13]

Bishop De Smedt, a gifted speaker, introduced the text to the assembly "with force and with fire" (as Yves Congar observed in his journal later that day).[14] Murray had prepared the first draft of De

---

[10] Regan, *Conflict and Consensus*, 36.

[11] Ibid., 82.

[12] John Courtney Murray "The Development of the Conciliar Document," in *Religious Liberty: An End and a Beginning*, ed. John Courtney Murray (New York: Macmillan, 1966), 15–42, at 16.

[13] Ibid., 17, 19.

[14] Yves Congar, *My Journal of the Council*, trans. Mary John Ronayne and Mary Cecily Boulding (Collegeville, MN: Liturgical Press, 2012), 433.

Smedt's report, and there are clear signs of his work in the version the fathers heard.[15]

De Smedt noted that "very many Fathers of the Council have very insistently asked that the Council openly expose and proclaim the right of man to religious freedom." In a remarkable statement, given the context of a presentation of a document being proposed for approval by a gathering of the world's bishops in ecumenical council, De Smedt acknowledged that "it is evident that certain quotations from the popes, because of a difference of words, can be put in opposition to our schema." He continued:

> But I beseech you, venerable fathers, not to force the text to speak outside of its historical and doctrinal context, not in other words, to make fish swim out of water. Let our document be studied as it stands. It is not a dogmatic treatise but a pastoral decree directed to men of our time. The whole world is waiting for this decree. The voice of the church on religious liberty is being waited for in universities, in national and international organizations, in Christian and non-Christian communities, in the papers, and in public opinion—and it is being waited for with urgency.[16]

When De Smedt finished, the bishop received a tremendous applause from his brother bishops.[17] Congar saw it as "a DECISIVE moment in the life of the Church AND OF THE WORLD."[18]

Following De Smedt's report, debate on the first three chapters of the schema on ecumenism (of which the religious freedom text was now considered chapter 5) commenced. It was a subject that clearly had the keen interest of the council fathers: though the official observers had been shocked at times by the bishops' tendency to leave the council floor half empty during formal debates at the moment the on-site coffee bars opened, on this occasion the bars were nearly deserted.[19]

[15] Pelotte, *John Courtney Murray*, 84; Regan, *Conflict and Consensus*, 37–45, 51.

[16] Cited in Xavier Rynne, *Vatican Council II* (New York: Farrar, Straus and Giroux, 1968), 237.

[17] Regan, *Conflict and Consensus*, 45.

[18] Congar, *My Journal of the Council*, 433.

[19] Soetens, "The Ecumenical Commitment of the Catholic Church," in Alberigo and Komonchak, 283; Joseph A. Komonchak, "Toward an Ecclesiology of Commu-

Though the debate of these days was officially limited to the first three chapters of the ecumenism schema (and therefore not on the religious freedom text), several council fathers did not hesitate to make reference to the latter. In the very first intervention, in fact, Cardinal Paul-Emile Leger suggested that the religious freedom schema should be considered as an entirely separate document. Other fathers suggested it would fit well within the context of the document, also under preparation, on the church in the modern world.[20]

Bishop Steven A. Leven, auxiliary of San Antonio, said in his intervention that it was unfortunate that some of the fathers "speak as if the whole doctrine of the freedom of conscience due every man, so clearly stated in *Pacem in Terris*, were offensive to pious ears; they prefer to censure the errors of non-Catholics whom they have never seen than instruct their own people."[21] Representing 110 of the 120 US bishops present, Chicago's Cardinal Meyer urged acceptance of chapter 5.[22]

On November 21, the council fathers voted in favor of accepting the first three chapters of the ecumenism text as a basis for discussion. The fourth and fifth chapters, on the Jews and on religious freedom, were not included in this vote, a fact that caused anxiety on the part of those who supported them; it meant the future of both texts was by no means assured. There was much discussion among some bishops and theologians that high ranking curial figures were pressuring the pope to delay discussion of the latter chapters, or even to scuttle them altogether.[23]

On November 29, the penultimate day of debate on ecumenism, Kansas City bishop Charles Helmsing concluded his intervention by suggesting it was time for an immediate vote on the fourth and fifth chapters. Many in the hall applauded his comment, but the moderators chose to ignore it. Several bishops, including many Americans,

---

nion," in *History of Vatican II*, vol. 4, ed. Giuseppe Alberigo and Joseph A. Komonchak (Maryknoll, NY: Orbis Books, 2003), 1–93, at 5.

[20] Regan, *Conflict and Consensus*, 49.

[21] Ibid.

[22] Komonchak, "The American Contribution," 9.

[23] Soetens, "The Ecumenical Commitment of the Catholic Church," in Alberigo and Komonchak, 287.

continued through the day to press for the vote, but by the end of the day they learned that the pope was in favor of postponing it until the following session.[24]

Adding to the tenor of the discussion was an article by John Courtney Murray that appeared in the November 30 edition of *America* magazine that "caused a great stir" among the council participants.[25] Murray insisted in the article that the church still did and ought to reject religious freedom based on the idea that people were not bound to God's law or that one religion was as good as another. But, he said, the decision for or against God was and had to be a personal decision, and so no coercion of any kind could legitimately be a part of it. He said that the "true tradition" regarding the relationship between church and state had been obscured in Europe for centuries by royal absolutism, but that it was currently lived in the United States: government as limited in competence to temporal matters of justice, peace, and freedom, and incompetent in religious matters. He said he wanted to see this idea enshrined by the council in its document on religious freedom.[26]

Despite all this, the second session of Vatican II came to an official close on December 4 without direct discussion of the religious freedom schema, with powerful curial figures (Ottaviani and Fenton central among them) marshalling their forces against it, leaving its fate up in the air.

Opposition and Support Crystalize

During the three months after the closing day of the second session, the SCU received 380 written interventions from various bishops on the ecumenism schema. Of these, 152 related directly to chapter 5. More than a third of those came from bishops of the United States.[27]

Prominent among these interventions were objections based on the classical thesis-hypothesis understanding of church-state relations.

---

[24] Regan, *Conflict and Consensus*, 49.

[25] Soetens, "The Ecumenical Commitment of the Catholic Church," in Alberigo and Komonchak, 286.

[26] John Courtney Murray "On Religious Liberty," *America* 109 (November 30, 1963): 704–6.

[27] Regan, *Conflict and Consensus*, 53.

These came especially from the bishops of Spain (whose national constitution presumed such an understanding). One Spanish bishop criticized the idea of religious freedom by citing Spanish dictator Francisco Franco; another flatly asserted that Pope John XXIII's support of religious freedom in *Pacem in Terris* was contrary to Catholic tradition; and still another made his point in an especially colorful and sarcastic intervention:

> Although more than ninety modern religions . . . founded by individual persons, agree without dissent both in denying the divinity of Christ and in rejecting the authority of the Church, this Church teaches solemnly through the Second Vatican Council that all these founders, and any other persons who . . . wish to found new religions impugning the divinity of Christ and the authority of the Church, enjoy the full right to do so.[28]

When it became clear to the American bishops—probably through communication with Murray, who was leading the task of evaluating all of the submitted interventions[29]—that the religious freedom text was receiving heavy criticism, they mobilized. Cardinal Meyer and Archbishop Sheehan wrote letters to Pope Paul insisting that the topic remain on the council's agenda. By the end of spring, the SCU had received over sixty letters from US bishops supporting the schema. Spellman's letter made ample use of a long memo that Murray had written for him in November on the value of the American constitutional system. Archbishop Alter, with whom Murray was in close contact, made a similar point in his own letter.[30]

Murray's work, however, was brought to a sudden, temporary halt on January 15, 1964, when he suffered a heart attack.[31] The SCU met for its plenary session February 27 through March 7, 1964, in Ariccia,

---

[28] Regan, *Conflict and Consensus*, 57, 63, 55.

[29] Evangelista Vilanova, "The Intercession (1963–1964)," in *History of Vatican II*, vol. 3, ed. Giuseppe Alberigo and Joseph A. Komonchak (Maryknoll, NY: Orbis Books, 2000), 347–490, at 434.

[30] Komonchak, "The American Contribution," 9, 11.

[31] Pelotte, *John Courtney Murray*, 85.

Italy. Though the text had not been directly discussed during the first session, the drafting committee used the additional time and the bishops' input to make revisions, though the result was not dramatically different from the previous version.

The degree of Murray's involvement in making the revision is unclear,[32] but his influence on it was not strong. This much is clear because by this time, a difference of approaches among those who supported the document was crystalizing. Murray favored a political-historical argument for religious freedom that was more accessible to unbelievers and relevant to the work of lawmaking in the modern world. Among European bishops and theologians (Yves Congar, for example) there was a preference for a more scriptural-theological approach. Murray complained privately that the text produced in March failed to "do justice to the political-social argument" and that the Europeans were "over-theologizing" the concept of religious freedom.[33]

In April, the council's Central Commission decided to separate the text on relations with the Jews (which had been included as chapter 4 of the schema on ecumenism) and the one on religious freedom (which had been chapter 5) from the ecumenism document. There was now, for the council's consideration, a decree on ecumenism, a declaration on the Jews and non-Christian peoples, and a declaration on religious freedom.[34] Cardinal Cicognani took the opportunity at this meeting to voice his puzzlement; it seemed "paradoxical," he said, "that the Catholic Church, the depository of the Truth and invested in the mandate of spreading and teaching this revealed creed, should presently . . . be championing these rights [to freedom] for other religions."[35]

Murray had his work cut out for him.

---

[32] Komonchak reports that as a result of his heart attack, Murray had "no role" in it. See "The American Contribution," 12. Vilanova says, "We know that he was able to share in the work" against the advice of doctors (434). Regan notes the plenary session and the revision work but does not mention Murray's participation.

[33] Komonchak, "The American Contribution," 13.

[34] Soetens, "The Ecumenical Commitment of the Catholic Church," in Alberigo and Komonchak, 282.

[35] Giovanni Miccoli, "Two Sensitive Issues: Religious Freedom and the Jews," in *History of Vatican II*, vol. 4, ed. Giuseppe Alberigo and Joseph A. Komonchak (Maryknoll, NY: Orbis Books, 2000), 95–193, at 103.

Chapter 14

Days of Wrath
(1964–1965)

As Murray's strength increased through the early months of 1964, so did his involvement with the conciliar work on religious freedom. Indeed, it was during the third session of the council that Murray's influence among its participants reached its apex.

Reading the Signs of the Times

In the summer of 1964, the American bishops' conference sent every member a copy of a new, long, and masterful article by Murray, just as they all were preparing for the third session of the council to begin. The article, which was surely some of Murray's clearest and best writing to date on the topic, was soon translated into four other languages and distributed in the fall to bishops throughout the world. It was published, with slight revisions, in December in *Theological Studies* and also appeared the following year in book form.[1]

The article began with a strong effort to present to two opposing sides of the matter as objectively and fairly as possible, calling them "the First View" and "the Second View." He noted that the fundamental idea of the First View (the classical thesis-hypothesis approach)

---

[1] John Courtney Murray, "The Problem of Religious Freedom," in *Religious Liberty: Catholic Struggles with Pluralism*, ed. Leon Hooper (Louisville, KY: Westminster/John Knox Press, 1993), 127–97; "The Problem of Religious Freedom," *Theological Studies* 25 (December 1964): 503–75; *The Problem of Religious Freedom* (Westminster, MD: The Newman Press, 1965).

was "the exclusive rights of truth. The whole system, especially the disjunction between thesis and hypothesis, derives from this concept." He acknowledged that many understood this view to be the formal teaching of the Catholic Church and said it "represents progress within the tradition, a clearer and less confused understanding of traditional principles."[2] The Second View, he said, was the result of recognition in modern times of humanity's growing "sense of personal freedom," as well as its growing "demand for political and social freedom."[3] As a result, the natural law at this moment in history called for a deepened respect for the religious freedom of all. Murray emphasized the limited powers of constitutional government and the distinction between "the sacred and the secular orders of human life."[4]

Murray reviewed, more clearly than he had in the past, the historical context in which the traditional approach had developed. He emphasized the historical circumstances in which Pope Leo XIII lived when he condemned religious freedom, explored Pope Pius's controversial address *Ci Riesce* at length, and characterized the teaching of John XXIII as "quietly bidding good-bye to both thesis and hypothesis in the sense of the *opinio recepta* [received opinion]."[5] "The task," he concluded, "is to discern the elements of the tradition that are embedded in some historically conditioned synthesis that, as a synthesis, has become archaistic. The further task is to discern the "growing end" of the tradition; it is normally indicated by the new question that is taking shape under the impact of the historical movement of events and ideas. There remains the problem of synthesis—of a synthesis that will be at once new and also traditional."[6]

It would, however, certainly exclude "the legal institution of religious intolerance, much less canonize it as a Catholic ideal."[7] The signs of the times, he insisted, using a phrase he repeated often throughout the essay, demanded it.

[2] Murray, "The Problem of Religious Freedom," in Hooper, 134, 136.
[3] Ibid., 137–38.
[4] Ibid., 144.
[5] Ibid., 178.
[6] Ibid., 188–89.
[7] Ibid., 189.

On September 21, Murray addressed the full body of US bishops as they met at the North American College in Rome. After he spoke for about an hour, Francis Connell and George Shea were each given a few minutes to voice their objections, and then the bishops voted to accept the revised religious freedom text (I will refer to it as Text 2) as a workable point of departure. Led by Cardinal Meyer, the bishops then prepared a carefully coordinated series of interventions giving voice to Murray's thinking that they intended to deliver on the council floor during the third session; they decided who would talk about what and in what order.[8] Fenton, who was also at the meeting, complained in his journal that there was "no trace of any desire [among the bishops] for debate or discussion. Connell and Shea walked out in disgust. I stayed until the end."[9]

The result, as Vatican II historian Joseph Komonchak has observed, was that "almost all of the contributions of US bishops in the debate [of the third session] and later in written comments bear the imprint of Murray's ideas and criticisms."[10] (Or, as Fenton put it in his journal at the time: "The US bishops have [illegible?] mouthed M's nonsense, as they have been told to do by Meyer."[11])

But the American bishops were not the only ones laying the groundwork for the debate ahead. The *Coetus Internationalis Patrum*, a study group of conservative-minded bishops, sent a strongly worded memo directly to the pope expressing their uneasiness about some of the schemas, specifically mentioning the declaration on religious liberty. Insisting that these schemas included statements contrary to church teaching and lacked a basis in sound Catholic theology and philosophy,

[8] Donald E. Pelotte, *John Courtney Murray: Theologian in Conflict* (New York: Paulist Press, 1975), 92–94; Fenton journal, "Journal of Trip to Rome, 1963–1965," box 1, folder 10, available at http://doc.wrlc.org/handle/2041/112137, September 25, 1964.

[9] Fenton journal, "Journal of Trip to Rome, 1963–1965," September 25, 1964, box 1, folder 10, available at http://doc.wrlc.org/handle/2041/112137.

[10] Joseph A. Komonchak, "The American Contribution to *Dignitatis Humanae*: The Role of John Courtney Murray, SJ," *U.S. Catholic Historian* 24, no. 1 (Winter 2006): 1–20, at 13.

[11] Fenton journal, "Journal of Trip to Rome, 1963–1965," September 25, 1964.

the group asked Paul VI to insist on unambiguous Catholic doctrine in the texts.[12]

Session Three Debate

On Wednesday, September 23, 1964, Bishop De Smedt presented Text 2 to the council fathers, now intended as an appendix to the schema on ecumenism rather than as the fifth chapter. Though the phrase "freedom of conscience" no longer appeared in the text, the primacy of the idea remained. The text spoke of the freedom to follow one's conscience as "the highest good proper to every person" and "a true and strict personal right." Indeed, the concept of "the right of the person" took a new prominence in Text 2 that had not been the case in Text 1.[13]

Finally, then, on September 23, formal conciliar debate on a proposed text on religious freedom began. The fact that nine of the ten speakers that day were cardinals is an indicator of its importance and urgency in the eyes of the fathers.

The prominent Cardinal Ruffini was first up. He made it clear that he saw little in the text that was acceptable, starting with the title. He said the title should refer to "religious tolerance," not religious freedom, since error has no rights and only the true religion has a right to freedom. Were the document to be accepted by the council, he pointed out, existing concordats the Holy See had established with Spain, Italy, Portugal, and the Dominican Republic (each of which established, to varying degrees, state support of Catholicism) would all need to be rescinded. "This is serious," Yves Congar wrote in his journal later that day. "The old warrior Ruffini has lost none of his punch."[14]

Boston's Cardinal Cushing spoke in the name of almost every American bishop. In a voice that was impressive and resounding,

---

[12] Evangelista Vilanova, "The Intercession (1963–1964)," in *History of Vatican II*, vol. 3, ed. Giuseppe Alberigo and Joseph A. Komonchak (Maryknoll, NY: Orbis Books, 2000), 433.

[13] John Courtney Murray "The Development of the Conciliar Document," in *Religious Liberty: An End and a Beginning*, ed. John Courtney Murray (New York: Macmillan, 1966), 15–42, at 20–21.

[14] Yves Congar, *My Journal of the Council*, trans. Mary John Ronayne and Mary Cecily Boulding (Collegeville, MN: Liturgical Press, 2012), 587.

but so heavily accented that his Latin was nearly unintelligible, he said, "Throughout its entire history, the Catholic Church has claimed freedom for itself within civil society and before the public authorities. . . . In our times the Church claims the same freedom within civil society for the other Churches and their members and indeed for every human being."[15] US Cardinals Meyer and Ritter also spoke in support of the document, though the latter with some reservations.

Ottaviani also spoke on Wednesday, offering a long list of problems with the text. It failed to teach that only those who embraced the true religion had a right to religious freedom, that the right to follow one's conscience was conditional on the fact that one's conscience was in accord with divine law, and that society had a right to limit one's freedom to follow one's conscience. He said the schema's assertion that civil government has no competence to make judgments about religious truth was contrary to the teaching of Pope Leo XIII.[16]

The archbishop of Santiago de Compostela offered an address that was "harsh and alarmed" that the proposed approach to religious freedom would stir up revolution and "unbridled license" in the church. The bishop of Toledo criticized religious freedom as "a doctrine novel to the Church." He pointed out that since we do not accept the spread of other errors that harm the common good, such as the licitness of suicide, neither should we accept religious error. "Do we perhaps think that religious errors are not as destructive?" he asked.[17]

As debate continued the next day, some of the schema's most ardent opponents took to the podium. Irish Cardinal Michael Browne insisted that the rights of one who has a correct conscience were not the same as those of someone with an erroneous conscience. Archbishop Parente said the document should not attempt to resolve questions that were still unresolved by theologians. Archbishop Marcel Lefebvre warned, "If this declaration is solemnly approved in its present form, great

---

[15] Giovanni Miccoli, "Two Sensitive Issues: Religious Freedom and the Jews," in *History of Vatican II*, vol. 4, ed. Giuseppe Alberigo and Joseph A. Komonchak (Maryknoll, NY: Orbis Books, 2003), 95–193, at 122.

[16] Richard J. Regan, *Conflict and Consensus: Religious Freedom and the Second Vatican Council* (New York: Macmillan, 1967), 75–76.

[17] Miccoli, "Two Sensitive Issues," in Alberigo and Komonchak, 111–12.

harm will be done to the respect the Catholic Church enjoys among all human beings and in all societies because of its unfailing love of the truth. . . . . The result will be the loss of many souls."[18]

The day also included an important intervention from Bishop Primeau of Manchester, New Hampshire, that strongly reflected Murray's thinking. Freedom of conscience (an internal matter) and religious freedom (a social matter) are, he said, indissoluble. Primeau also pointed out that there are two kinds of rights: the right to do something and the right to demand that others not do something. Religious freedom, he said, falls in the second category; it is immunity from any legal or social force in religious matters. He said it was in this sense that the schema proclaimed religious freedom for all people, an approach which avoided any danger of suggesting that one religion is as good as another.[19]

The third day of debate on religious freedom included an intervention from Archbishop Karol Wojtyla of Krakow, Poland. In language that would be quite recognizable to anyone who would later follow his teaching following his 1978 election as pope (as John Paul II, he would become known as a prominent defender of religious freedom across the globe), Wojtyla commented that the document, as it stood, really was directed to two audiences—the "separated brothers" of the Protestant communities and rulers of nations—and so suggested it be divided into two different documents. He emphasized the close connection between freedom and truth, and he insisted that religious freedom was "a fundamental right" that "must be strictly observed by all, especially those who govern."[20]

Another important intervention was that of Bishop Carlo Colombo. During the first session of the council, Colombo had participated as Cardinal Montini's *peritus*. Now that Montini was pope and Colombo had been consecrated bishop, his words were given careful attention. Colombo told the bishops that religious freedom should be understood as resting on three doctrinal principles: the right of every person to

[18] Regan, *Conflict and Consensus*, 77; Miccoli, "Two Sensitive Issues," in Alberigo and Komonchak, 113.

[19] Regan, *Conflict and Consensus*, 79, 94.

[20] *Acta Synodalia* III/2, 530–32. My translation from the Latin.

seek and express the truth, the obligation of every person to follow a certain conscience, and the free and supernatural nature of the act of faith. The duty of the state, he maintained, is to protect religious freedom. "Unless we have this declaration," Colombo said, "there can be no dialogue with men of good will."[21]

After Colombo, debate formally concluded, though some thought this came prematurely. Many fathers soon submitted written interventions on the schema. An important one from Cardinal Patrick O'Boyle of Washington contained ideas (clearly Murray's) that would appear in the subsequent revision of the schema. Religious freedom is a right, he said, because governments are incompetent to make judgments about both religious truth and personal conscience. He said there is a distinction between society and the state, and the protection of the public order—the role of government—is only a part of the common good of society. Therefore, the state can limit religious freedom only to the extent that it protects public order, not to protect the general common good.[22]

Another written intervention was particularly colorful in expression. Bishop Leo Lemay, the apostolic vicar of the Northern Solomon Islands, criticized the classical formulation of the church-state problem, saying that its careful construction

> not only does not open the windows of the Church; it has closed the windows and doors of the Church for centuries. Ought we not, venerable Fathers, be speaking to the world? . . . If so, then let us return that kind of talk to the dusty and musty libraries of the past century. . . . If we are not to disgrace our Church, the Church of Christ, in the eyes of the world, let us abandon language derived from scholastic theology; if we do not, then let us be silent.[23]

By this point, midway through the third session of the council, the frustration among conservatives with the general direction the council

---

[21] Regan, *Conflict and Consensus*, 84–85; Miccoli, "Two Sensitive Issues," in Alberigo and Komonchak, 130–33.

[22] Regan, *Conflict and Consensus*, 88–90, 94.

[23] Miccoli, "Two Sensitive Issues," in Alberigo and Komonchak, 124.

had long been taking was coming to a head. It was during this period of time that Yves Congar wrote in his journal of comments made to him by a fellow *peritus*: "On all sides [in the Roman congregations] he hears bitter complaints about 'this cursed Council' which is 'ruining the Church'. . . . They say: if only it was over, and these bishops went back home!!!"[24] Around the same time, Cardinal Siri recorded in his own journal the response he offered the pope when he asked Siri when the council should end. "Immediately if possible," the cardinal told Paul VI, "for the air at the Council is harmful." In their frustration, many of the more conservative prelates had begun to exert pressure on the pope to steer things in a more agreeable direction.[25]

"The News Burst like a Bomb"

On October 9, as the SCU was working hard to revise the draft, Cardinal Bea received a letter from Cardinal Felici, secretary general of the council, informing him that the pope had asked for work on the religious freedom schema to be handed over to a new mixed commission, in the hopes of reaching conciliation and compromise. Bea was to pick four SCU members to join four TC members, whom the letter named. Among the latter, three—Cardinal Browne, Archbishop Lefebvre, Father A. Fernandez (master general of the Dominicans and a Spaniard)—were adamant opponents of the schema. The fourth, Bishop Colombo, supported it.

"The news exploded like a bomb upon the little world of the Council, with much noise and smoke," one observer later wrote, noting that the American bishops were particularly upset.[26] Besides three of the four TC members being utterly opposed to a teaching on religious freedom, the directive went against conciliar rules and also suggested that Cardinal Bea could not manage the work of his own commission. "These events," Congar journaled, "are contributing to the maintenance of a

---

[24] Congar, *My Journal of the Council*, 606.

[25] Miccoli, "Two Sensitive Issues," in Alberigo and Komonchak, 171.

[26] Robert Rouquette, "La Concile, Le Second Mois de la Troisième Session," *Études* (December 1964): 715–32, at 720.

kind of distrust with respect to the people of the Curia, who are felt to be trying to sabotage the Council."[27]

On October 11, a large group of cardinals met at Cardinal Frings's apartment to address the matter. Gathered in the room were some of the most prominent and influential prelates of the church: Frings, Leger, Konig, Alfrink, Ritter, Dopfner, and others. Together they crafted a letter of protest. Saying they viewed the call for a mixed commission with "great distress," the cardinals wrote of their "very great disquiet" at the development and asked "very insistently" that the religious freedom schema be left in the hands of the SCU. Twelve cardinals signed it and added a note that further signatures would be added soon. It was delivered to the pope the same day.[28] By that time, Paul VI had also received strong letters from Cardinal Bea and from the secretary of state official Msgr. Willebrands, who warned that Browne, Lefebvre, and Fernandez would work "to thwart fruitful work in the mixed commission."[29]

On October 16, word came that the recently announced approach was terminated. The schema would remain fully under the SCU's jurisdiction and there would be no mixed commission to prepare a new text, though three TC members—Browne, Fernandez, and Colombo (now no Lefebvre)—would "study" what the SCU produced in a consultative role.[30]

An "American" Text

With the crisis—another moment when the future of what eventually became the Decree on Religious Freedom was in doubt—averted, the SCU returned to the task of revising the draft. Murray was named "first scribe," or primary author, of the subcommittee handling the

---

[27] Congar, *My Journal of the Council*, 618.

[28] Miccoli, "Two Sensitive Issues," in Alberigo and Komonchak, 187–88.

[29] Ibid., 183–86.

[30] Pelotte, *John Courtney Murray*, 95; Regan, *Conflict and Consensus*, 95–99, see also 203. Miccoli makes a good case that the mixed commission was Cardinal Felici's doing rather than the pope's, that the latter had intended everything to stay with SCU but to involve others in the work (172ff).

work, and his impact on the next draft would prove decisive.[31] The text that resulted, officially known as the *textus emandatus* (I will refer to it as Text 3), was dramatically different from its predecessor, and the hand of John Courtney Murray in preparation of this text was obvious to anyone familiar with his work.

Now intended as a separate council document, independent of the one on ecumenism, Text 3 was about four thousand words in length (twice that of the previous draft), with eighty percent of its content new. Human dignity (rather than "right conscience") was identified more clearly as the foundation of the right to religious freedom, and emphasis now was heavily on religious freedom as a juridical concept. Where the previous texts had insisted on the right of an individual personally to follow his or her conscience but avoided the question of whether a government had a right to repress public manifestations of religious belief, Text 3 insisted on the freedom of all from any constraints or restraints on their religious practice by government. (This, of course, sounded very much like the American constitutional concept of limited government.) The transition to this emphasis in the religious freedom document, which Murray would later call "a decisive moment in the legislative history of the text," would remain through all subsequent revisions. One result was that where a loophole for the traditional thesis-hypothesis thinking might have been found in the previous texts, no such loophole existed in the new text. Text 3 also included several references to contemporary circumstances and a long portion on the historical development of the church's teaching, especially in the nineteenth century, a particularly recognizable Murray contribution.[32]

By this time, two camps had clearly developed among those who supported religious freedom at the council. Murray's approach (and therefore that of most American bishops) was political, sociological, juridical, and historical. The alternative—called the "French" approach—preferred a more clearly theological and scriptural grounding for religious freedom. Supporters of the latter saw Text 3 as distinctly "American" and were uncomfortable with the idea that "the experience

[31] Pelotte, *John Courtney Murray*, 94.
[32] Murray, "The Development of the Conciliar Document," 27–37, 42.

of one country should be considered as universal."[33] Bishop De Smedt, a close ally of Murray's, wrote to him privately that he was "disappointed by the very juridical way in which you treat the question."[34] Congar wrote in his journal: "Hardly anything is left of the previous text. . . . I find that there is a certain superficiality in this approach. The redactors (especially Pavan and Murray) have no idea of the difficulties that their text will raise. The BIBLICAL part is mediocre."[35]

Despite such misgivings, the SCU accepted Text 3 on October 24.

Black Thursday

Text 3 was distributed to the council fathers on Tuesday, November 17—four days before the session was set to conclude—with voting on the schema set for Thursday. On Wednesday, Cardinal Felici, secretary general of the council, announced that because Text 3 was so different from the previous version, many fathers felt they needed more time to consider it; therefore, before the next day's vote on the document, there would first be a vote on whether the vote should take place.[36]

On Thursday, as Bishop De Smedt prepared to step to the podium to introduce the text to the fathers, council president Cardinal Eugene Tisserant engaged in a quick conversation with those among the other nine presidents who were seated directly around him. He then announced brusquely and unexpectedly that the presidents had decided that there would be no vote on the religious freedom document this session. De Smedt would introduce the text and discussion could begin the following year; any fathers who wished should submit their written observations about the text to the SCU by January 31, 1965.[37]

[33] Komonchak, "The American Contribution," 16, quoting Dominque Gonnet, *La Liberté Religieuse à Vatican II: La contribution de John Courtney Murray, SJ* (Paris: Les Editions du Cerf, 1994), 181.

[34] Ibid., 16.

[35] Congar, *My Journal of the Council*, 626.

[36] Pietro Pavan, "Declaration on Religious Freedom," in *Commentary on the Documents of Vatican II*, Volume 4, ed. Herbert Vorgrimler, trans. Hilda Graef, W. J. O'Hara, and Ronald Walls (New York: Herder and Herder, 1969), 49–86, at 54.

[37] Luis Antonio G. Tagle, "The 'Black Week' of Vatican II (November 14–21, 1964)," in *History of Vatican II*, vol. 4, ed. Giuseppe Alberigo and Joseph A. Komonchak (Maryknoll, NY: Orbis Books, 2003), 387–453, at 391–92.

This meant the new text would not be formally "in possession" by the council and could therefore be removed from the agenda without ever coming to a vote by the body of bishops.

After the already troublesome issues of postponement and delay, Tisserant's announcement was a shock. An immediate wave of indignation and frustration swept the council floor. Bishops and theologians were suddenly—as *Newsweek* reported it a few days later—"milling about the floor like frantic brokers at the stock exchange. Bitterness burned through a babble of tongues."[38]

Cardinal Meyer, who was one of the council presidents but had not been privy to Tisserant's quick conversation with those around him before the announcement, became visibly upset. He banged his fist on the table and asked Cardinal Ruffini, seated beside him, if he'd been aware the announcement was coming. The satisfied smile that Ruffini offered Meyer in reply frustrated the Chicago prelate all the more. Meyer next approached Tisserant but soon dismissed him, audibly calling him "hopeless." A group of agitated bishops and theologians quickly coalesced around Meyer in the center of the Basilica. Even those who had misgivings about the text felt they were being treated dismissively, even contemptuously, and resented it. "They are treating us like children," one bishop complained aloud.[39]

"Let's not stand here talking. Who's got some paper?" Bishop Francis Reh, rector of the North American College, called out.[40] Soon a handwritten petition to the pope, calling for a reversal of the move, was being passed around the floor of Saint Peter's for the bishops to sign. *Beatissime Pater*, it began, *reverenter sed instanter, instantius, instantissime petimus* ("Most Holy Father, respectfully but urgently, very urgently, most urgently we ask").[41]

As the tense situation played out, Bishop De Smedt had little choice but to proceed with introducing the text. A speaker of lesser skills might have ended up ignored in the confusion, but De Smedt quickly

[38] "The Bitter End," *Newsweek*, November 30, 1964, 68.
[39] Robert Rouquette, "Les Derniers Jours de la Troisième Session," *Études* (January 1965): 100–120, at 113.
[40] "The Bitter End," 68.
[41] Pavan, "Declaration on Religious Freedom," in Vorgrimler, 54.

grabbed the attention of the hall and his address was interrupted repeatedly by vigorous applause from his frustrated audience, at times more than once in the same sentence. Richard J. Regan captures well the drama of the moments following De Smedt's speech:

> When he had concluded his report, wild applause, the longest and most sustained of the Council, was accorded his speech. Some of the bishops even stood up in order to clap more vigorously, and two Moderators openly joined the cheering forbidden by the rules. Cardinal Dopfner, the Moderator of the day, made no attempt to stop the sustained applause. In any event, he was powerless to control this display of enthusiasm.[42]

When Dopfner finally tried to thank De Smedt for his report, he made several unsuccessful attempts before he was able to finish a sentence.

"Thwarted once again in their desire to have a vote," John Coleman, SJ, has written, "they voted by vigorously clapping their hands."[43] In his careful account of the day's events and their background, Luis Antonio Tagle explains, "The thunderous and prolonged applause that interrupted his speech became an occasion for assembly members to manifest their shock, frustration, disbelief, and anger at the turn of events."[44]

The hastily prepared petition quickly gathered hundreds of signatures on the council floor—one account says a thousand in half an hour.[45] Cardinals Meyer, Leger, and Ritter took it immediately and directly to the pope, who received them promptly, though they had no appointment. Unwilling to embarrass Tisserant, the pope upheld the decision, promising that religious freedom would be, if at all possible, the first item on the agenda when the fourth session of the council opened in the fall of 1965. Later in the day, at a previously scheduled

---

[42] Regan, *Conflict and Consensus*, 113. Tagle, too, calls the applause "the longest applause accorded an intervention during the Council" (Tagle, "The 'Black Week' of Vatican II," 101).

[43] John Coleman "The Achievement of Religious Freedom," *U.S. Catholic Historian* 24, no. 1 (Winter 2006): 28.

[44] Tagle, "The 'Black Week' of Vatican II," 401.

[45] Rouquette, "Les Derniers Jours de la Troisième Session," 113.

gathering, another group of cardinals appealed to Paul VI to reconsider his decision, but to no avail.

The day would come to be known as "Black Thursday." Murray later called it the "Day of Wrath."[46] Years later, Donald E. Pelotte would call it "another day of defeat for religious liberty."[47]

The session formally concluded on November 21 with the approval and promulgation of the Dogmatic Constitution on the Church, the Decree on Eastern Churches, and the Decree on Ecumenism. In a letter he sent to the pope the previous day, Bishop De Smedt wrote,

> I fear that, during the fourth session, the declaration on religious freedom will be the object of sabotage maneuvers similar to those it has encountered during these three sessions. Like most of the bishops, I leave Rome profoundly saddened and disheartened by the barely tolerable methods that are constantly being employed by certain influential members of the minority and that have created an extremely serious prejudice to the honor and prestige of Holy Church.[48]

"Largely Murray's Work"

In December, just after the close of the third session, Murray suffered his second heart attack. But when the SCU subcommittee charged with further revisions of the religious freedom schema gathered on February 18, 1965, he was there. Since the close of the third session, 218 written interventions on the schema were submitted by bishops to the SCU.[49] (One not-so-subtle indicator that Murray's key role in the drafting was commonly known was an Italian bishop's complaint of the text's Latin being marked by too much transliteration from "a certain modern language."[50])

---

[46] John Courtney Murray, "This Matter of Religious Freedom," *America* 112 (January 9, 1965): 40–43.

[47] Pelotte, *John Courtney Murray*, 96.

[48] Tagle, "The 'Black Week' of Vatican II," 402.

[49] Regan, *Conflict and Consensus*, 117.

[50] Ibid., 121.

Yves Congar had become more involved in the process by this point as the leader of a small group of biblical specialists working on a scriptural section for the schema. Expressing the "French" approach, Congar wanted religious freedom to be "seen through the history of salvation." "THAT," he wrote in his journal on February 19, "is what will be spoken of, from this point onwards."[51] Murray's contributions on historical context were reduced now, and the section explaining the nineteenth-century development of church teaching was cut. His arguments from natural law were still there, but new sections on Scripture, salvation history, and pastoral considerations, prepared by Congar, were added. The SCU, meeting in plenary session February 28 through March 6, approved the newly revised text.

Because Pope Paul had made clear that he wanted to see the text before the council fathers did, it was sent to him on March 20.[52] On May 6, in a meeting with Bishop Colombo and Cardinal Felici, the pope handed the men several handwritten pages of his own observations about the text. His comments emphasized the foundations of religious freedom in natural law and positive law and the incompetence of the state on religious matters. In other words, they sounded a lot like the thinking of John Courtney Murray.

On the evening of the same day, Colombo met with Murray and passed the pope's observations on to him. Murray, of course, welcomed the input but worried about how Congar would react. After the meeting, Colombo summarized his discussion with Murray in a letter to the pope. He included a copy of Murray's article of the previous summer and concluded his letter, "Father Murray is a very open, solid, and good man: I think that a conversation with him would help Your Holiness to know personally a very valuable man who could be of help in American circles."[53]

After reviewing Paul VI's reactions, the subcommission decided to eliminate Congar's scriptural section from the draft. The SCU unani-

---

[51] Congar, *My Journal of the Council*, 728. See also 733–34.

[52] Riccardo Burigana and Giovanni Turbanti, "The Intercession: Preparing the Conclusion of the Council," in *History of Vatican II*, vol. 4, ed. Giuseppe Alberigo and Joseph A. Komonchak (Maryknoll, NY: Orbis Books, 2003), 453–615, at 538.

[53] Ibid., 542n207. See the full text of Colombo's letter here.

mously approved the changes and sent the text on to the pope and the Central Commission.[54] In June 1965, this new version of the religious freedom schema—the *textus re-emendatus* (which I will call Text 4), was sent to the council fathers around the world, followed by a long report on the topic that was "largely Murray's work."[55]

[54] Ibid., 543–44.

[55] Komonchak, "The American Contribution," 17. See also Regan, *Conflict and Consensus*, 121; Gilles Routhier, "Finishing the Work Begun: The Trying Experience of the Fourth Period," in *History of Vatican II*, vol. 5, ed. Giuseppe Alberigo and Joseph A. Komonchak (Maryknoll, NY: Orbis Books, 2006), 49–184, at 64n46.

Chapter 15

The American Contribution
to the Council
(1965)

A s the fourth and final session of the Second Vatican Council
opened on September 14, 1965, the feast of the Triumph of
the Cross, two opposing and irreconcilable "sides" were lined
up against one another on the issue of religious freedom, with the
conservative side, led by Ottaviani, a powerful minority. Both sides
saw resolution of the question as a matter of speaking the truth about
God and the church and morality, which meant that, for these men, the
stakes could not be higher. All knew that the matter would be decided
definitively in the weeks ahead. Indeed, they had been preparing in-
tensely for the debate almost from the moment that the previous year's
session had closed.

Battle Stations

In January 1965, Murray had published another article in *America*
magazine that was much commented on; it was soon translated and
published in Italian and German periodicals as well.[1] A few months
later, *L'Osservatore Romano* published an article by the prominent
French theologian Charles Boyer that defended the classical thesis-
hypothesis approach.

---

[1] Gilles Routhier, "Finishing the Work Begun: The Trying Experience of the
Fourth Period," in *History of Vatican II*, vol. 5, ed. Giuseppe Alberigo and Joseph A.
Komonchak (Maryknoll, NY: Orbis Books, 2006), 49–184, at 64n47.

The new religious freedom text the bishops had received in June (Text 4) had been closely scrutinized by supporters and opponents alike for months. Cardinal Ritter had written a letter to the entire American episcopate, calling for their support of the religious freedom schema.[2] The *Coetus Internationalis Patrum*, meanwhile, had invited the world's bishops to provide their Roman addresses during the next session in order to receive advice on how to vote.[3] And Cardinal Siri had written directly to the pope complaining that, if promulgated, the new document would "especially benefit religious indifferentism."[4]

The Canadian bishops, who had paid special attention to Murray's work, prepared among themselves a sequence of interventions in favor of the schema for the fourth session.[5] And less than two weeks before the session's opening, the Yugoslavian bishops published a joint pastoral letter to their faithful declaring their support for religious freedom.[6]

In late summer, an exchange between representatives of the two dominant approaches among religious freedom supporters played an important role in the debate. French theologian Fr. Guy de Broglie, who favored religious freedom but wanted to see it expressed in more scriptural and theological terms than Murray's approach provided, prepared a long critique of the current text. He sent a copy to Murray, who responded with a long and careful rejoinder. One of the French bishops included both of these texts in a dossier he sent to the entire French episcopate and included a conclusion of his own that came down in favor of Murray's way of thinking. This dossier played an important role in reconciling the two sides and opening the French bishops to accepting Murray's more juridical approach. Congar's willingness to support the approach was also instrumental.[7]

---

[2] Donald E. Pelotte, *John Courtney Murray: Theologian in Conflict* (New York: Paulist Press, 1975), 96.

[3] Routhier, "Finishing the Work Begun," in Alberigo and Komonchak, 61.

[4] Ibid., 46, 47n114.

[5] Ibid., 66n55.

[6] Ibid., 76n98.

[7] Richard J. Regan, *Conflict and Consensus: Religious Freedom and the Second Vatican Council* (New York: Macmillan, 1967), 127–29.

During this same period, Murray carried on a respectful correspondence with Cardinal Browne, a leader of the conservative opposition to the religious freedom document. Murray explained the text and defended its importance. But knowing how unlikely it would be to win the cardinal's agreement, he also added:

> There is an old folk-ballad among us about a boy who was treed by a bear (it is of Negro origin, as many are). The refrain runs thus: "O Lord, if you can't help me, for heaven's sake don't help the bear." It comes to mind as an expression of my hope in this matter: if your Eminence does not find it possible, in conscience, to come out in favor of the schema, I hope that you will not find it necessary, in conscience, to come out against it![8]

As he had the previous fall, Murray worked with the American bishops to prepare a set of coordinated interventions for session four, covering all the important points at issue.[9]

"Voices of the Bishops . . . Thoughts of Murray"

On September 15, the debate on Text 4 began. Bishop De Smedt presented an introductory report, again prepared with extensive consultation with Murray.[10]

The first council father to speak was Cardinal Francis Spellman, who offered his strong support through an intervention that had been prepared by Murray.[11] Cardinals Cushing and Ritter followed with their support. Over the next several hours, a series of American prelates also spoke in favor of the document. American bishop after American bishop offered interventions that clearly reflected Murray's thinking. One bishop in the hall commented, "The voices are the voices of

---

[8] Pelotte, *John Courtney Murray*, 98.

[9] Ibid., 66n54.

[10] Regan, *Conflict and Consensus*, 132; Routhier, "Finishing the Work Begun," in Alberigo and Komonchak, 6, 5n51.

[11] Regan, *Conflict and Consensus* 132; Routhier, "Finishing the Work Begun," in Alberigo and Komonchak, 67n61.

the United States bishops; but the thoughts are the thoughts of John Courtney Murray!"[12]

The day also included several voices of opposition, including the influential Cardinals Ruffini and Siri. Ruffini repeated the classical approach that the state was obligated, through its officials, to worship God according to the Catholic religion. He noted the great benefits that Catholicism brings to society, offering as his first example of such benefits chastity. Siri warned of religious indifferentism and suggested again that the religious freedom schema contradicted the teaching of several popes.[13]

On the second day of debate, Cardinal Jaeger spoke in the name of 150 bishops in favor of the draft. His intervention offered impressive responses to many of the criticisms that had been raised by its opponents.[14]

The third day included several noteworthy interventions. Cardinal Franjo Seper (who would one day succeed Ottaviani as head of the Congregation for the Doctrine of the Faith) offered his strong support.[15] Cardinal John Heenan, the archbishop of Westminster, criticized the thesis-hypothesis approach, noting that it was absurd to speak of truth or error having rights, since only persons have rights. He said the traditional approach was inconsistent: the church cannot appeal to "the rights of truth" when Catholics are in the majority and use it to suppress the freedom of non-Catholics, and when Catholics are in the minority, demand freedom for Catholics.[16]

The Spanish Cardinal Modrego y Casaus said the schema "certainly contradicts . . . the explicit teaching of the Roman pontiffs up to and including John XXIII." Another Spaniard, Velasco, said it "perverts the doctrine taught for centuries by the magisterium of the Church." Ottaviani again offered his opposition, maintained that the teaching of the schema were "for the most part contrary to common teaching"

---

[12] Pelotte, *John Courtney Murray*, 98; Joseph A. Komonchak, "The American Contribution to *Dignitatis Humanae*: The Role of John Courtney Murray, SJ," *U.S. Catholic Historian* 24, no. 1 (Winter 2006): 1–20, at 17n48.

[13] Regan, *Conflict and Consensus*, 133.

[14] Ibid., 136–7; Routhier, "Finishing the Work Begun," in Alberigo and Komonchak, 72.

[15] Regan, *Conflict and Consensus*, 140.

[16] Ibid., 141; Routhier, "Finishing the Work Begun," in Alberigo and Komonchak, 73.

and called for a revision that would bring it "in accord with the earlier teaching of the Catholic Church."[17]

Speaking on behalf of "all of the observers of the Council," Bishop Charles Maloney, the auxiliary bishop of Louisville, offered strong support for the schema. He noted wryly that the council fathers who were wrong about this issue had "a right to speak because of their dignity as persons, not because of the truth or falsity of their statements."[18]

By the end of the day on Friday, as the bishops adjourned for the weekend, the direction the debate was taking was still unclear. There was by no means any certainty that the schema on religious freedom would be accepted by the council. The *peritus* Albert Prignon would later write in his journal of this day, "Chance meetings with bishops and theologians in St. Peter's showed that minds were wavering. Several bishops said openly that they did not know what they ought to think and how they should cast their votes."[19] Some thought if a vote had been called, many hundreds of fathers would vote against it, and one rumor suggested that one thousand were ready to reject it.[20] In the midst of the uncertainty, some of the leading bishops who had been supportive of the schema the previous year—Cardinals Lercaro and Leger, for example—had stepped back and kept quiet this time around. The French bishops, who supported religious freedom but thought the schema was too juridical in approach and lacked a sound scriptural foundation (that is to say, it reflected Murray's thinking), were tepid in their support.[21] Pope Paul VI, who had made no secret of the fact that he wanted the declaration, told Cardinal Suenens that he had been very impressed with the arguments of the leaders of the opposition.[22]

Bogged Down

Monday morning, September 20, brought the fourth day of debate on Text 4. The first to speak was Cardinal Joseph-Charles Lefebvre

---

[17] Routhier, "Finishing the Work Begun," in Alberigo and Komonchak, 71.

[18] Regan, *Conflict and Consensus*, 143.

[19] Routhier, "Finishing the Work Begun," in Alberigo and Komonchak, 79.

[20] Ibid., 80, 83n131, 85.

[21] Ibid., 80–81.

[22] Ibid., 81.

(not to be confused with Archbishop Marcel Lefebvre who was adamantly opposed to the document). This Lefebvre used his intervention
to respond carefully and effectively to six objections repeatedly raised
by opponents of the religious freedom schema.[23] Then came Baltimore's Cardinal Sheehan, who spent his time at the podium addressing criticism that the document was unfaithful to Catholic doctrine.
He provided a careful and systematic review of the teaching of past
popes—clearly Murray's work—in "the ardent hope . . . that the
fathers will approve the schema almost unanimously."[24]

There followed a rather remarkable series of interventions on behalf
of the document. Cardinal Josef Beran took his place before the fathers.
During the 1940s, Beran had been imprisoned by the Nazis in the
Theresienstadt and Dachau concentration camps. After four years of
freedom, during which he had been named archbishop of Prague, Beran
was imprisoned in 1949 by the Communist regime and remained so
until 1963. Since his release, he had been forbidden by his government
from exercising his ministry. As he stood on the floor of the council
that fall of 1965, he had just moved to Rome a few months earlier, in
exchange for concessions from his government for more freedom for the
church in Czechoslovakia, and had been named a cardinal by Paul VI.

Standing for the first time before his brother bishops, who knew well
the suffering he had endured for his fidelity to the church, Beran reminded them of the burning of the Czech priest Jan Hus in the fifteenth
century and the forced conversions of Czech Protestants in the seventeenth century. These events, he said, "left a certain wound hiding in the
hearts of the people" and damaged the church's credibility. He called
for repentance on the part of the church and said that "the principle of
religious freedom and freedom of conscience must be set forth clearly
and without any restriction flowing from opportunistic considerations."[25]

---

[23] Ibid., 89.

[24] Ibid., 90.

[25] Regan, *Conflict and Consensus*, 145; Routhier "Finishing the Work Begun,"
in Alberigo and Komonchak, 90; Xavier Rynne *The Second Session: The Debates and
Decrees of Vatican Council II, September 29 to December 4, 1963* (New York: Farrar,
Straus, & Co., 1964), 463; (Beran died in Rome in 1969 and is buried in the grottoes
of Saint Peter's Basilica. His cause for canonization is under investigation.)

Following Beran, Cardinal Joseph Cardijn took his place before the bishops. Cardijn was the founder of the Young Christian Workers, an impressive movement that at that moment was made up of nearly two million members in almost seventy countries around the globe. Pope Paul had named Cardijn a cardinal, in recognition of his remarkable work, in the recent consistory alongside Beran. Cardijn, too, spoke in favor of the religious freedom schema.

As if that were not enough, the next speaker was Cardinal Stefan Wyszynski, archbishop of Warsaw and primate of Poland, who also had suffered imprisonment—in his case for three years—under the Communists. He too spoke in favor of the schema.[26]

Despite these dramatic statements, there still was a great deal of disarray on the issue. Several interventions were highly negative. Archbishop Lefebvre bitterly condemned the schema, saying that the principle of religious freedom "is not one conceived . . . by the church." The sharp conflict even generated some apathy on the part of some council fathers. Many of the official Protestant observers began to sense that the schema might not succeed. Historian Gilles Routhier has written of this point, "The debate seemed to have bogged down, and no one could find a way ending it." The next morning's headline in the *New York Herald Tribune* would read "Vatican Council near Crisis over Religious Liberty Issue."[27]

On Tuesday morning, Pope Paul (who was just a month away from a historic visit to the United Nations headquarters in New York City) summoned the council leadership to his apartment to say he thought it was time for a preliminary vote on the schema.[28]

As the morning's interventions began, Cardinal Enrico Dante, whose face was well-known through his longtime role as papal master of ceremonies, suggested that the teaching of the schema sounded like echoes of the French Revolution. Cardinal Journet, a noted theologian who was trusted by the more conservative among the fathers, spoke in favor of the schema; his intervention surely went a long way toward

[26] Regan, *Conflcit and Consensus*, 145.
[27] Ibid., 94, 96, 101, 96n177.
[28] Ibid., 150.

reassuring some among the fathers who felt uneasy about the schema because of charges of unfaithfulness to traditional teaching.[29]

At 10:30 a.m., after four interventions, Cardinal Agagianian took to the podium and asked the fathers to indicate by a standing vote whether they thought it was time to close discussion. Nearly every one of the fathers stood. Bishop De Smedt offered a summary and closing remarks, and then the fathers were asked to vote on whether the current text should be taken as the basis for a definitive declaration after further amendments, to be subsequently approved by council. The voting resulted in 1,997 in favor, 224 against, and 1 invalid, a decisive victory for supporters of the document. When the tally was announced, the bishops responded with applause in the hall.[30] The next morning's *London Times* called the vote "a great event in the history of Catholicism and in the history of freedom."[31]

September 22 brought a few more interventions on the schema as were permitted by council rules. One of them was from Archbishop Karol Wojtyla, who spoke in favor of the document in the name of the bishops of Poland, saying that religious freedom was in harmony with both human reason and divine revelation.[32] Bishop Ancel offered an important intervention in the name of more than one hundred French bishops, saying that a person could not authentically seek the truth if he were not free of all coercion; therefore religious freedom was founded on our responsibility to seek the truth.[33] The Italian *peritus* Pietro Pavan later wrote, "Thus ended a debate that was perhaps the most violent ever to have taken place in the aula. It had been rich in dramatic moments."[34]

[29] Routhier, "Finishing the Work Begun," in Alberigo and Komonchak, 102–3.

[30] Regan, *Conflict and Consensus*, 149–50.

[31] Routhier, "Finishing the Work Begun," in Alberigo and Komonchak, 107n223.

[32] Regan, *Conflict and Consensus*, 151.

[33] Ibid., 151–52.

[34] Pietro Pavan, "Declaration on Religious Freedom," in *Commentary on the Documents of Vatican II*, Volume 4, ed. Herbert Vorgrimler (New York: Herder and Herder, 1969), 49–86, at 57.

"Champagne, Friends, Smiles"

Having received another 201 written interventions following the close of debate, the SCU subcommission set to work on final revisions on September 23. In an audience that Bishop De Smedt had with Paul VI on September 30, the pope told De Smedt, "This is a major document. It establishes the attitude of the church for several centuries. The world is waiting for it."[35]

For a while, John Courtney Murray played a central role in the revision work. His fellow *peritus* Yves Congar described him during this period as "very much overloaded with responsibility for various matters." But on October 5, he was rushed to the hospital with a collapsed lung. When Congar visited him two days later, Murray, with oxygen tubes in each nostril, tried to provide his feedback on the current text to Congar. Congar—who had had his disagreements with Murray about the text—found the ideas important enough that he immediately passed them on to SCU officials. Congar wrote that evening, "Thus Fr. Murray was ill, and seriously so, at the moment when a text was being finalised which had been, to a great extent, his work. He himself told me that he is taking this mystically, in the sense of the cross, and that he is perhaps more useful to the text in bed and powerless, than up and active."[36]

Murray was not the only one on whom the process was taking a serious physical toll. Congar was utterly exhausted, writing in his diary during this time that he could barely stand up and felt like a tree that had been struck by lightning. He also described his fellow *peritus* Henri de Lubac on October 4, 1965, as being "very tired, crushed."[37] Fenton, too, who had suffered two of his own heart attacks during the years of the council, wrote repeatedly in his own diary of his exhaustion.

In Murray's absence, the revisions to the document brought a shift in tone, closer to the "French" approach, adding more emphasis to revelation and theology, including a preface on revelation, written by Congar. Murray's more constitutional and legal approach, however, was

[35] Yves Congar, *My Journal of the Council* (Collegeville, MN: Liturgical Press, 2012), 795.

[36] Ibid., 803, 806.

[37] Ibid., 801, 798.

not eliminated. Also added to assuage conservative fears of indifferent-ism was a more explicit acknowledgment that the Catholic Church was the true church founded by Christ. (When it was made public, the *New York Herald Tribune* headline would read: "Council Revision Makes It a Duty of All to Be Catholic."[38]) The text—officially called the *textus recognitus* (I will call it Text 5)—was accepted by the subcommittee on October 9 and distributed to the council fathers on October 22. The *Coetus* immediately sent around papers intended to demonstrate the document contradicted the Bible and church teaching.[39]

Bishop De Smedt introduced the text to the council fathers on Oc-tober 25. The voting on its various parts took place over the following two days. After that, the SCU received more than 4,000 petitions for amendments. The SCU met again in plenary session November 8 and 9, with Murray again present (though Congar wrote of Murray in his journal: "he spoke in a voice that seemed like that of a ghost, and as though it came from the other side of the veil").[40] The team made final revisions to the text, which were mostly insignificant, and then Text 6—the final one—was distributed to the council fathers on November 17, with voting scheduled for two days later.

On November 18, 1965, John Courtney Murray was invited to con-celebrate Mass with Pope Paul VI in St. Peter's Basilica, along with several others representing the many council *periti*. It was a remarkable moment, considering that exactly one decade earlier, Murray had been, under Vati-can pressure, forbidden to write or publish his work. A friend later wrote, "In private, the event was celebrated with champagne, friends, smiles—and toasts that were really prayers for the future of a beloved Church in a kind of turmoil that its servant could only wish to prove holy."[41]

On Friday, November 19, the council fathers voted first on various parts of the document—with each vote resulting strongly in favor—and finally on the whole text. The latter vote was 1,954 in favor, 249 against, and 13 invalid.[42]

---

[38] Routhier "Finishing the Work Begun," in Alberigo and Komonchak, 117.
[39] Ibid.
[40] Congar, *My Journal of the Council*, 834.
[41] Pelotte, John Courtney Murray, 100.
[42] Regan, *Conflict and Consensus*, 166–67.

Disappointed and frustrated by this and other aspects of the council's conclusions, Joseph Fenton did not even bother to stay in Rome for the final flurry of promulgations of several major texts and the historic concluding ceremonies of the council. He left early, in late November, noting in his journal, "It was a great mistake to let [*Gaudium et Spes*, the Constitution on the Church in the Modern World], the one on religious liberty, and the one on non-Christian religions, get by the council."[43]

On December 7, 1965, in the final public session, the formal vote on the Declaration on Religious Freedom was 2,308 in favor, 70 against, and 8 invalid. On that day, Pope Paul VI formally proclaimed it (along with the Decree on the Ministry and Life of Priests, the Decree on the Church's Missionary Activity, and the Pastoral Constitution on the Church in the Modern World) as documents of the council. The Second Vatican Council's closing ceremonies took place the following day.

Dignitatis Humanae

The approved document is around 3,300 words in Latin, excluding footnotes (and closer to five thousand in English), composed of an introduction and two chapters. The introduction acknowledges a growing demand for freedom in society in modern times and professes faith in the Catholic Church as the "one true religion" founded by Christ. Significantly, it states explicitly that the council "intends to develop the teaching of recent popes on the inviolable rights of the human person and on the constitutional order of society."

In chapter 1, the council "declares that the human person has a right to religious freedom" and "further declares that [this right] is based on the very dignity of the human person." The chapter notes repeatedly that religious freedom is comprised primarily of the right to "immunity from external coercion in religious matters" (also phrased as "the right not to be hindered" in religious matters and "the right not to be prevented" from religious practice).

The second chapter insists that while the right to religious freedom can be known by human reason, it is also "rooted in divine revelation."

[43] Fenton journal, "Journal of Trip to Rome, 1963–1965," box 1, folder 10, available at http://doc.wrlc.org/handle/2041/112137, November 26, 1965.

Acknowledging that it is not explicitly expressed in Scripture, the council taught that revelation "throws light on the general principles" on which religious freedom is based—especially on the fact that each person's act of faith must be made with freedom. The chapter also strongly defends the church's right to freedom in carrying out its own mission in society.

Murray himself, less than a year later, would point to "three doctrinal tenants" declared by *Dignitatis Humanae*: "the ethical doctrine of religious freedom as a human right (personal and collective); a political doctrine with regard to the functions and limits of government in matters religious; and the theological doctrine of the freedom of the Church as the fundamental principle in what concerns the relations between the Church and the socio-political order."[44] By any account, its teaching is, in terms of Catholic doctrine, historic.

---

[44] John Courtney Murray, "Religious Freedom," in *The Documents of Vatican II*, ed. Walter M. Abbott (New York: Guild Press, 1966), 672–74, at 672–73.

Chapter 16

After Vatican II
(1965–1967)

O n December 8, 1965—the day the Second Vatican Council went
from being a current event to being history—John Courtney
Murray had 616 days left to live. Twenty months later, the story
of his life and remarkable achievements came to a quick and tragic halt
in a New York City taxi cab. With the close of the council, then, the
rest of his story is, sadly, short.

Cardinal Cushing and Contraception

In May 1966, the legislature and governor of Massachusetts approved a repeal of the law that prohibited the distribution of contra-
ceptives in the state. In truth, Massachusetts was the very last of the
fifty states to make this move, so there is perhaps a certain inevitability
here. Still, the shift was a historic marker in the nation's social, cultural,
religious, and legal history, and John Courtney Murray played a key role
in it. His involvement was directly related to his thinking on religious
freedom and his work on the topic at the Second Vatican Council.

More than two years earlier, in the first week of December 1964,
Democratic State Congressman Michael Dukakis, a Catholic, had filed
a bill that would lift the state's ban on the sale of birth control and
on doctors even offering information about it to their patients. That
the Archdiocese of Boston and its powerful leader, Cardinal Richard
Cushing, would become involved in the legislative process on this was
nearly a given.

Seventeen years earlier, in 1948, a voter referendum that would allow the distribution of birth control devices to married women "for the protection of life or health" had been defeated. Then-Archbishop Cushing had been instrumental in the outcome. Indeed, his vocal opposition—which he expressed from the cathedral pulpit, in his archdiocesan newspaper the *Pilot*, and on the radio—was based explicitly on the classical Catholic understanding of the church-state relationship that Ottaviani and Fenton would later use to condemn the thinking of Murray on religious freedom and which the council fathers would reject. "In March [1948]," historian Seth Meehan has written, "[Cushing] referred to the birth control restrictions as being a 'unique advantage' for Massachusetts, for they explicitly tied the state's law to God's law." Cushing insisted that members of his flock defend the state law because it was "absolutely immoral." (He also characterized it as antisocial and antipatriotic.) When it came time to vote, a majority of the members of that flock had complied.[1]

By late 1964, Cushing, now a cardinal, had only grown in public prestige among both Catholics and non-Catholics in Massachusetts. US Senator Edward Kennedy had recently praised him on the Senate floor, saying, "No one, in my judgment, has made a greater contribution to racial and religious understanding in my part of the nation than Cardinal Cushing." In February 1964, the *New York Times* had published a flattering profile of Cushing, calling him the "Symbol of 'New Boston.'" And when it came to Dukakis's bill, Planned Parenthood League of Massachusetts executive director Hazel Sagoff privately acknowledged in December that the "political realities in Massachusetts are that unless a bill is approved by the Cardinal, it gets voted down by the legislature."[2]

Faced with a new battle on the issue, Cardinal Cushing approached Murray for his input. By late 1964, of course, Cushing was quite familiar with Murray's thinking on religious freedom and church-state relations. Indeed, Cushing had cooperated with his brother bishops in

[1] Seth Meehan, "From Patriotism to Pluralism: How Catholics Initiated the Repeal of Birth Control Restrictions in Massachusetts," *The Catholic Historical Review* 96, no. 3 (July 2010): 470–98, at 475, 490.

[2] Ibid., 470–71, 492, 474.

carrying out Murray's coordination of their interventions on the council floor and personally read conciliar interventions that were largely Murray's own work.

Murray provided Cushing with a long memo on the topic. It stated in the first sentence that "Catholics may and should approve" the amendment. Distinguishing between public morality and private morality, he argued that contraception fell into the latter category, particularly because the practice was approved by many religious groups. He cited religious freedom as a "secondary" argument, saying that the law should not restrain a person from acting according to conscience, unless the action were "against the public peace, against public morality, or against the rights of others." Murray added that contraception remained a moral issue for Catholics "to be decided according to the teaching of the Church. Because contraception is made legal it is not therefore made moral. . . . Catholics might well take this public occasion to demonstrate that their moral position is truly moral, that is, it is adopted freely, out of personal conviction and in intelligent loyalty to their Church."[3]

A legislative panel hearing to address the bill seeking to repeal the state contraception ban opened on March 2, 1965, and at the invitation of the Joint Committee on Public Health, Cushing was "the hearing's star witness." As it turned out, Cushing himself was unable to attend because he was recovering from surgery, but his testimony was read in his name by his attorney. Murray himself had written the first draft of this statement, and the final text that was read in Cushing's name followed Murray's draft "nearly word for word" with "no significant changes."[4]

The position laid out in Cushing's statement was that he could not endorse the proposal, but he had no wish to oppose it. "Catholics do not need the support of civil law to be faithful to their own religious convictions and they do not seek to impose by law their moral views on other members of society." Outside of the hearing, he would later

---

[3] John Courtney Murray, "Memo to Cardinal Cushing on Contraception Legislation," in *Bridging the Sacred and the Secular: Selected Writings of John Courtney Murray, SJ*, ed. J. Leon Hooper (Washington, DC: Georgetown University Press, 1994), 81–86.

[4] Ibid., 470, 471, 496.

say, "It's up to [the legislature]. It's their business." The *Boston Globe*'s front page headline the following day announced: "Cardinal Relaxes Anti-Birth Law Stand."[5]

To the surprise of many, Massachusetts rejected the bill by a close vote in August, thanks to the opposition of some vocal opponents of it.

The issue was raised again in the legislature in April 1966. This time, with the Declaration on Religious Freedom now official church teaching, Cushing was willing not only not to interfere with the passage of the law but also to actively endorse the bill. It passed and became law the following month.[6]

Cushing's position through this process "was critical to the long-term success of the legislation." The Planned Parenthood League of Massachusetts acknowledged in an internal document after the fact that the "Catholic understanding of religious liberty for persons of all faiths" had been the "most important" factor in this "great victory."[7]

"Tired of the Whole Subject"

In the spring of 1966, *Time* magazine noted that no one in America received more honorary academic degrees that year than Murray. During graduation season, he received honorary degrees from six institutions: Yale, Columbia, Fordham, Gonzaga, Fairfield, and Detroit Universities.[8]

Also that spring, Murray was appointed director of the John LaFarge Institute, which had been founded two years earlier by the editors of the Jesuit journal *America*. It was an ecumenical effort that gathered academic, social, and political leaders to study interracial relations and racial discrimination, as well as a wide range of other social issues, including poverty, war and peace, censorship, business ethics, and the arts.[9]

[5] Ibid., 471, 497, 472.

[6] Ibid., 473.

[7] Ibid., 474, 497.

[8] "Colleges: Kudos," *Time*, June 24, 1966, http://content.time.com/time/subscriber /article/0,33009,835814,00.html.

[9] Donald E. Pelotte, *John Courtney Murray: Theologian in Conflict* (New York: Paulist Press, 1975), 101; David W. Southern, *John LaFarge and the Limits of Catholic Interracialism, 1911–1963* (Baton Rouge: Louisiana State University Press, 1996), 356;

Murray was invited by President Lyndon Johnson's administration to serve as a member of a presidential advisory committee on conscientious objection. When that committee addressed the issue of selective conscientious objection—that is, the right of a person to conscientious objection not only to war in general but also to a particular war for particular reasons about why or how it was being fought—only two out of twenty-four members voted in favor of acknowledging such a right. Murray was one of the two.[10]

In October 1966, when a fellow Jesuit wrote to Murray with questions about the issue of religious freedom and his work at the council, Murray responded by referring him to another scholar. "I myself," he wrote, "have given up the idea of writing a history of the Declaration on Religious Freedom. I have done six articles on various theoretical aspects of the declaration and I am frankly tired of the whole subject."[11]

In May 1967, in an address to a group of priests in Toledo, Ohio, Murray talked about the changes brought about by the Second Vatican Council and paid special attention to contraception and recent disclosures about the majority and minority reports of the special commission assigned by Pope Paul VI to study the issue. (The encyclical *Humanae Vitae* was still over a year away.) "The church," Murray told the priests,

> reached for too much certainty too soon, it went too far. Certainty was reached in the absence of any adequate understanding of marriage. This, many would hold—I would hold—is today no longer theologically tenable. . . . It is also psychologically untenable.
>
> In the absence of an adequate understanding of marriage, there was an inadequate understanding of the marital act and an inadequate understanding of the total situation of the problem of reproduction, especially in its demographic dimension. Also there was an inadequate understanding of the authority of the church as exercised in the field of natural morality.[12]

Thomas W. O'Brien, *John Courtney Murray in a Cold War Context* (Landham, MD: University Press of America, 2004), 101.

[10] Pelotte, *John Courtney Murray*, 102.

[11] Ibid., 101.

[12] "Appendix: Toledo Talk," in Hooper, 334–41, at 336.

Heart problems persisted and became more serious. After an initial hospitalization in 1953 for extreme exhaustion resulting from cardiac problems, he'd had his first heart attack in 1958, another in 1962. Chronic back problems became nearly debilitating; there were times he was in such pain that he could not genuflect at Mass and bowed only with difficulty. He also suffered from angina pain.[13]

On Wednesday, August 16, 1967, while on his way in a taxi cab from his sister Katherine's house in Queens to his office at the LaFarge Institute in Manhattan, he was struck by another heart attack, and this one would take his life. The cab driver took him to a hospital, where he was pronounced dead. He was sixty-two years old.

Murray's funeral was celebrated at the Church of St. Ignatius in New York City. Cardinals Spellman and Cushing were in attendance, and Fr. Walter Burghart preached the homily. "Untold Catholics," Burghart told the assembly, "will never sense that they live so gracefully in this dear land because John Murray showed so persuasively that the American proposition is quite congenial to the Catholic reality." He was buried at the Jesuit cemetery at Woodstock College, where he had taught for thirty years.[14]

Connell: "Not in the Least"

Just three months prior to Murray's death, one of his early intellectual adversaries, the Redemptorist priest and CUA professor Francis Connell, died on May 12, 1967, at age seventy-nine. In an interview just a few months before his death, Connell insisted that the council had done little to alter his views, not because he disagreed with its teaching, but because its teaching had not touched directly on his disputes with Murray, and he briefly praised the theologian against whom he had written many letters to Vatican authorities.

---

[13] Mark Williams, "Memories of 'Uncle Jack': A Nephew Remembers John Courtney Murray," in Mark Bosco and David Stagaman, *Finding God in All Things: Celebrating Bernard Lonergan, John Courtney Murray, and Karl Rahner* (New York: Fordham University Press, 2007), 92–98, at 94, 97.

[14] Ibid., 92, 98. Williams notes that the Woodstock campus is today the state of Maryland's Job Corps Center, but the Jesuit cemetery remains intact; Michael P. Sheridan, "Of Many Things," *America* 117, no. 10 (September 2, 1967): 208.

Recalling these disputes, Connell said, "I said that the *ideal* situation is where the State recognizes the Catholic Church as the one, true Church. Father Murray believed that the Church and State should be separated. I insisted that in the ideal situation they should not be separated, even though in particular conditions they might be."[15]

Asked, "Does the *Decree on Religious Liberty* of the Second Vatican Council cause you to change your views?" Connell replied: "Not in the least, because it says nothing about this question." Insisting that the document had neither condemned nor approved the union of church and state, he said,

> The *Decree on Religious Liberty* is an excellent statement, and I am in full agreement with it. Father Murray deserves great credit for the labor he put into it. Remember that religious freedom is by no means freedom of conscience. That phrase was left out of the document completely. Religious liberty is based on the dignity of man and this means that man should not be subjected to any coercion on the part of civil authority in religious matters, either to do what is against his conscience or to refrain from doing what his conscience dictates, unless public order is concerned.
>
> My controversy with Father Murray was on Church-State, and that is not the same as religious liberty. *Ideally*, the Church should be recognized by the State and its rights acknowledged. There should be a union in this sense. . . . In the *practical* order, I have always held that it is best, even in Catholic states, to have a recognition of all people. Every man should be allowed to do what his conscience dictates. My argument was based on the principle of the greater good. Nowadays, it is based on human dignity.[16]

Fenton: Disappointment and Frustration

Like Murray, Fenton had been plagued by heart problems during the years of the council. In December 1963, after heart attacks in May and September of that year, he had resigned as editor of the *American*

---

[15] Patrick Granfield, "An Interview with Father Connell," *AER* 157 (August 1967): 74–82, at 81.

[16] Ibid., 81–82.

Ecclesiastical Review after twenty-five years in the position and also from the teaching post he had held at The Catholic University of America for just as long.[17] He was assigned as pastor of St Patrick's parish in Chicopee Falls, Massachusetts, in his home diocese of Springfield, where he spent the remainder of his life.

Fenton remained disappointed with much of the teaching that the council produced. He did some preliminary planning for a book he expected to call *To Be a Priest in the Church after Vatican II,* in which he intended to "make some necessary but rather strong comments" about several council documents.[18] He planned another book on ecclesiology, writing, "My main thesis will be that the Catholic theology on the Church has been improved but in no way changed by the Council. . . . The Council . . . minimized or glossed over the fact that the Church faces opposition, not just from hostile individuals, but from the 'world.'"[19] But he never completed either manuscript or published any other book.

Fenton returned to Rome three times in the years just after the council, socializing during each trip with Cardinal Ottaviani. During each, he was also able to join small groups for semiprivate audiences with Pope Paul VI, and on each occasion, the pope singled Fenton out for some personal attention.

Fenton suffered several more heart attacks through the winter of 1968–1969 before finally succumbing to another while he slept in his Chicopee Falls rectory on July 7, 1969, at age sixty-three.[20] His death came less than two years after Murray's.

Ottaviani: An Old Soldier

As the Second Vatican Council drew to a close, Cardinal Alfredo Ottaviani was already recognizing that he had decisively lost many of

---

[17] Fenton journal, "Journal of Trip to Rome, 1963–1965," box 1, folder 10, available at http://doc.wrlc.org/handle/2041/112137, September 24, 1963; *AER* 150 (January 1964): 1.

[18] Fenton journal, "Journal of Trip to Rome, 1963–1965," October 26, 1965.

[19] Fenton journal, "Journals of the 23rd, 25th, 26th, and 27th Trips to Rome, 1966," box 1, folder 11, available at http://doc.wrlc.org/handle/2041/112138, November 23, 1968.

[20] Obituary, *Springfield Union,* July 8, 1969, 27, cited by Wikipedia, http://en.wikipedia.org/wiki/Joseph_Clifford_Fenton.

the battles he had fought, and he seemed ready to accept the losses in a spirit of humility and loyalty to the Church. In October 1965, on the day before his seventy-fifth birthday, Ottaviani told a journalist

> I am the soldier who guards the gold reserve. . . . If you tell an old soldier that the laws are going to change, it is clear that, being an old soldier, he will do everything he can to keep them from changing. But if the laws change anyway, God will certainly give him the strength to come to the defense of the new treasure in which he believes. Once the new laws become the treasure of the Church, enriching the gold reserve, then there is only one principle that counts: to serve the Church. And this service means being faithful to its laws.[21]

Ottaviani retired from his post at the Congregation for the Doctrine of the Faith on January 8, 1968. He spent much of his time in the years that followed working to support the orphanage that he had founded decades earlier in Frascati. He also remained engaged in developments in the church following the council. When Pope Paul VI promulgated the reformed Roman Missal in 1969, he joined another prominent curial cardinal, Antonio Bacci, in penning a critical commentary on the new liturgy, which the two presented to the pope.[22] Paul VI maintained a warm and respectful relationship with Ottaviani, once visiting him in the hospital as he recuperated from eye surgery. In 1976, he sent Ottaviani a warm letter of congratulations to mark his sixtieth anniversary of priestly ordination.[23]

But Ottaviani survived Paul VI (and Murray, Fenton, and Connell), finally passing away on August 3, 1979, at the age of eighty-eight. Pope John Paul II chose to personally preside and preach at his funeral Mass.

---

[21] Henri Fesquet, *Le Journal du Concile* (Foulcalier: Robert Morel, 1966), 1019. Author's translation from the French.

[22] Alfredo Ottaviani, Antonio Bacci, et al., *The Ottaviani Intervention: Short Critical Study of the New Order of Mass* (Rockford, IL: TAN Books, 1992).

[23] Alberto Royo Mejía, "Recordando al Cardenal Alfredo Ottaviani a los 30 años de su fallecimiento," at Temas de Historia de la Iglesia, http://infocatolica.com/blog /historiaiglesia.php/recordando-al-cardenal-alfredo-ottaviani-1.

Conclusion

A Call for a Little More Doctrinal Humility

"John Courtney Murray is the most significant Catholic theologian the church in the United States has ever produced," Bishop Robert McElroy has written.[1] Some have gone even further, to say he was "the finest"[2] and "the most outstanding"[3] we have had. Agree with that or don't, but there is no room for argument that he was and remains the most significant. Through his work, Murray prompted a historic rethinking of Catholic doctrine that came to be expressed in a historic conciliar document. As we have seen, that did not come easily. *Dignitatis Humanae* was incredibly controversial at the council, and its opponents engaged in numerous ploys and machinations to keep it from reaching completion and approval.

Though the United States had not yet celebrated its bicentennial at the time, Murray brought about, against powerful opposition, the first significant contribution of the unique experience of the American people to the doctrinal life of the Catholic Church. The Declaration on

---

[1] Robert W. McElroy, "He Held These Truths," *America* 192, no. 4 (February 7, 2005), available at http://www.americamagazine.org/content/article.cfm?article_id=3995.

[2] Joseph A. Komonchak, "John Courtney Murray," in *The Encyclopedia of American Catholic History*, ed. Michael Glazier and Thomas J. Shelley (Collegeville, MN: Liturgical Press, 1997), 993–96, at 996.

[3] Charles Curran, *American Catholic Social Ethics: Twentieth-Century Approaches* (Notre Dame, IN: University of Notre Dame Press, 1982), 232.

Religious Freedom clearly represents what may be called—as one bishop who was there put it—the "American contribution to the Council."[4]

There is a sentence I encountered in my research that struck me as quite fascinating, even unsettling. It was written by Murray's old theological nemesis, Joseph Fenton, in that article from the June 1951 issue of the *AER*—the same article that Cardinal Ottaviani cited and quoted in his major March 2, 1953, address at the Lateran University in Rome. In that article, Fenton took careful aim at Murray's work and explained why he thought it to be quite mistaken. In the midst of this explanation Fenton composed the sentence that struck me quite forcefully.

"In the event that Fr. Murray's teaching is true," Fenton wrote— and remember who is writing: a well-regarded scholar, professor of theology at the US bishops' own prestigious university on these shores, editor of a prominent theological journal, and the man later chosen to serve as the expert theological advisor during the Second Vatican Council to Ottaviani himself, head of what we call today the Congregation for the Doctrine of the Faith—"In the event that Fr. Murray's teaching is true," he wrote, "then it would seem that our students of sacred theology and of public ecclesiastical law have been sadly deceived for the past few centuries. . . . It is hard to believe that any Catholic could be convinced that an entire section of Catholic teaching about the Church itself could be so imperfect."[5]

Fenton was not the only one who found this hard to believe. Ottaviani saw Murray's distinction between the timeless aspects of Catholic doctrine and the historically conditioned aspect as dangerous, suggesting that those who proposed such ideas were laying down the very "weapons of truth" entrusted to the church by God. He said it was clear that Murray was questioning "a certain and incontestable truth,"

---

[4] Donald E. Pelotte, *John Courtney Murray: Theologian in Conflict* (New York: Paulist Press, 1975), 100.

[5] Joseph Fenton, "The Status of the Controversy," *AER* 124 (June 1951): 452, 456. Elsewhere Fenton had observed, "The truth that the state, like every other human society, is objectively obligated to worship God according to the one religion He has established and commanded is so obviously a part of Catholic doctrine that no theologian has any excuse to call it into question." See Fenton, "The Relation of the Christian State to the Catholic Church," *AER* 123 (September 1950): 214–18.

and that the principles on which this truth was based were "firm and immovable."[6]

We could multiply the quotations like this, as we have seen already. And they came from good people who were gifted in many ways, who knew their theology well, who prayed, who loved God and God's people and God's church. These men had been entrusted by the church with the role, the charism, of teaching and defending Catholic doctrine—which is, to be clear, the good news of Jesus Christ for the salvation of the world.

Let's also be clear: that good news and the doctrinal truths that express it do sometimes meet with opposition from "the world." Though Fenton probably had an exaggerated sense of the ongoing conflict between the world and the Gospel, it would be foolish to suggest that such conflict does not exist, and it would be mistaken to suggest that Catholics ought not to offer that Gospel anyway—with courage, respect, and love—to the world.

But in this case, these men—Fenton, Ottaviani, Gilroy, Lefebvre, and many others—got it wrong. The "truths" Murray questioned were not as "immovable" as they seemed to be. One thing Murray's opposition got wrong, in other words, was that one had to choose between either Vatican II's document on religious freedom or earlier ones from Pope Leo XIII and Pius X that they believed it clearly contradicted.

Catholic theologians today can offer a quick and easy answer to that quandary, of course: a development of doctrine took place. But that does not resolve the matter. The fact is, what we recognize today within the church to be an authentic development of doctrine looked a lot to some people in 1954 (when Murray was silenced) and 1964 (when the council fathers debated his ideas) like a *contradiction* of doctrine.

Francis Connell put the matter perhaps better than he realized in a July 1951 article that also opposed Murray. He said Murray's work marked a "very definite and radical departure from what has hitherto been commonly regarded as Catholic doctrine."[7] Murray did depart

---

[6] Alfredo Ottaviani, "Discorso di Sua Eccelenza il Cardinale Alfredo Ottaviani sul Tema 'Chiesa e Stato,'" (CUA archives, NCWC/USCC file).

[7] Francis Connell, "The Theory of the Lay State," *AER* 125 (July 1951): 7–18, at 17–18.

from what had been *commonly regarded* as Catholic doctrine, and he knew it; but he insisted that it wasn't the *doctrine* he was questioning but rather the historically conditioned *expression of* it. All it took was for Murray and others (Congar and Pavan, Bea and De Smedt, for example) *to consider the question of religious freedom from a different perspective, to ask the questions about it in a different way and by taking into consideration different premises and new circumstances*, to make what seemed to be a contradiction into a legitimate development.

The problem is, of course, that it is sometimes hard to tell the difference. One thing the story of John Courtney Murray and his struggle for the truth about religious freedom teaches us is that understanding the truth about God and God's revelation to humanity is sometimes a struggle. That revelation and what it means in the circumstances of our day (and any day) is not always clear and easily discernible—even by those whose job it is to discern it.

In a church that is so often divided by theological, political, and cultural differences, it seems important that we remember that. It seems that we need to be a little more patient with one another and cautious about how certain we are in our judgments about our own thinking and that of others. Our love for God, for God's truth, for God's church, and for all people demands it.

Bibliography

Primary Sources

"Animadversiones de Schematibus Reformandis a Commissionibus Propriis Secundum Propositiones Commissiones de Concilii Laboribus Coordinandis." Archives of the Archdiocese of New York, S/C 110, folder 1, Cardinal Spellman, Literary Works, Vatican Council II Correspondence.

Cardinal Francis Spellman Correspondence: to Amleto Cicognani, February 11, 1963; to Msgr. Fearns, March 31, 1953; to John Courtney Murray, April 9, 1963; to Cardinal Alfredo Ottaviani, April 5, 1954. Archives of the Archdiocese of New York, S/D-3, folder 6. Cardinal Spellman Correspondence with the Hierarchy. Apostolic Delegate to the US.

Congar, Yves. *My Journal of the Council.* Translated by Mary John Ronayne and Mary Cecily Boulding. Collegeville, MN: Liturgical Press, 2012.

Fenton, Joseph Clifford. *Joseph Clifford Fenton Diaries, 1948–1966.* Washington, DC: The American Catholic History Research Center and University Archives, Catholic University of America. Box 1. Available at http://doc.wrlc.org/handle/2041/112117/browse?type=dateissued.

Fenton to Murray correspondence, March 31, 1953. John Courtney Murray Papers. Box 1, folder 70. Washington, DC: Georgetown University Library, Special Collections Research Center.

Hall, Frank A. to Monsignor Howard J. Carroll correspondence, March 20, 1953. Hall to Carroll correspondence, March 27, 1953. American Catholic History Research Center and University Archives, The Catholic University of America, United States Conference of Catholic Bishops Office of the General Secretary, Series 1 (General Administration Series). Box 14, folder 12.

John Courtney Murray, "Notes from which Fr. Murray spoke in McMahon Hall, Catholic University, March 25, 1954." The Reverend John Courtney Murray, SJ, Papers, Georgetown University Special Collections Research Center, Series 4, box 5, folder 402.

———. "Notes on the Theory of Religious Liberty." April 1945 Memo to Archbishop Edward Mooney. Washington, DC: Georgetown University

Library, Special Collections Research Center. John Courtney Murray Papers. Box 7, file 555.

Ottaviani, Alfredo. "Discorso di Sua Eccelenza il Cardinale Alfredo Ottaviani sul Tema 'Chiesa e Stato.'" American Catholic History Research Center and University Archives, The Catholic University of America, United States Conference of Catholic Bishops Office of the General Secretary, Series 1 (General Administration Series). Box 14, folder 12.

Vatican Council II, *Acta Synodalia* III/2, pp. 530–32.

Works by John Courtney Murray

Bridging the Sacred and the Secular: Selected Writings of John Courtney Murray, SJ. Edited by J. Leon Hooper. Washington, DC: Georgetown University Press, 1994.

"The Church and Totalitarian Democracy." *Theological Studies* 13 (December 1952): 525–63.

"Contemporary Orientations of Catholic Thought on Church and State in the Light of History." *Theological Studies* 10 (June 1949): 177–234.

"The Court Upholds Religious Freedom." *America* 76 (March 8, 1947): 628–30.

"Current Theology: Christian Co-operation." *Theological Studies* 3 (September 1942): 413–31.

"Current Theology: Freedom of Religion." *Theological Studies* 6 (March 1945): 85–113.

"Current Theology: Intercredal Co-operation: Its Theory and Its Organization." *Theological Studies* 4 (June 1943): 257–86.

"Current Theology: On Religious Freedom." *Theological Studies* 10 (September 1949): 409–32.

"Dr. Morrison and the First Amendment." *America* 78 (March 6, 1948): 627–29.

"Dr. Morrison and the First Amendment: II." *America* 78 (March 20, 1948): 683–86.

"For the Freedom and Transcendence of the Church." *American Ecclesiastical Review* 126 (January 1952): 28–48.

"Freedom of Religion, I: The Ethical Problem." *Theological Studies* 6 (June 1945): 229–86.

"Governmental Repression of Heresy." *Proceedings of the Third Annual Convention of the Catholic Theological Society of America*, 26–98. Bronx: Catholic Theological Society of America, 1948.

"Leo XIII on Church and State: The General Structure of the Controversy." *Theological Studies* 14 (March 1953): 1–30.

"Leo XIII: Separation of Church and State." *Theological Studies* 14 (June 1953): 145–214.

"Leo XIII: Two Concepts of Government." *Theological Studies* 14 (December 1954): 551–67.

"Leo XIII: Two Concepts of Government II: Government and the Order of Culture." *Theological Studies* 15 (March 1954): 1–33.

"On Religious Liberty." *America* 109 (November 30, 1963): 704–6.

"On the Structure of the Church-State Problem." In *The Catholic Church in World Affairs*, edited by Waldemar Gurian and M. A. Fitzsimons, 11–32. Notre Dame, IN: University of Notre Dame Press, 1954.

"The Problem of Religious Freedom." *Theological Studies* 25 (December 1964): 503–75.

The Problem of Religious Freedom. Westminster, MD: The Newman Press, 1965.

"The Problem of 'The Religion of the State.'" *American Ecclesiastical Review* 124 (May 1951): 327–52.

"Religious Freedom." In *The Documents of Vatican II*, edited by Walter M. Abbott, 672–74. New York: Guild Press, 1966.

Religious Liberty: An End and a Beginning. Edited by John Courtney Murray. New York: Macmillan, 1966.

Religious Liberty: Catholic Struggles with Pluralism. Louisville, KY: Westminster/John Knox Press, 1993.

"Reversing the Secularist Drift." *Thought* 24 (March 1949): 36–46.

"Separation of Church and State." *America* 76 (December 7, 1946): 261–63.

"Separation of Church and State: True and False Concepts." *America* 76 (February 15, 1947): 541–45.

"St. Robert Bellarmine on the Indirect Power." *Theological Studies* 9 (December 1948): 491–535.

"This Matter of Religious Freedom." *America* 112 (January 9, 1965): 40–43.

We Hold These Truths: Catholic Reflections on the American Proposition. New York: Sheed & Ward, 1960.

Secondary Sources

Abbott, Walter M. "Cardinal Cushing." *America* 108 (June 15, 1963): 864–67.

———. "Truth First and Always," *America* 108 (March 30, 1963): 434–46.

Alberigo, Giuseppe, and Joseph A. Komonchak, eds. *History of Vatican II*, Volumes 1–5. Maryknoll, NY: Orbis Books, 1995–2006.

Appleby, R. Scott and John Haas. "The Last Supernaturalists: Fenton, Connell, and the Threat of Catholic Indifferentism." *U.S. Catholic Historian* 13, no. 2 (Spring 1995): 23–48.

Auchincloss, Douglas. "To Be Catholic and American." *Time* (December 12, 1960). http://content.time.com/time/subscriber/article/0,33009,871923,00 .html.

Bévenot, Maurice. "Thesis and Hypothesis." *Theological Studies* 15 (1954): 440–46.

"The Bitter End." *Newsweek* (November 30, 1964): 68.

Blanshard, Paul. *American Freedom and Catholic Power*. Boston: Beacon Press, 1949.

Bosco, Mark and David Stagaman, eds. *Finding God in All Things: Celebrating Bernard Lonergan, John Courtney Murray, and Karl Rahner*. New York: Fordham University Press, 2007.

Bowie, W. Russell. "Protestant Concern over Catholicism." *American Mercury* 69 (September 1949): 261–73.

Buckley, William F. "Nihil Obstat." *National Review* 10 (January 28, 1961): 56–57.

Butterfield, William. "Co-operation with Non-Catholics." *The Clergy Review* 22 (April 1942): 160–65.

Campion, Donald R. and Daniel J. O'Hanlon. "Council Jottings." *America* 109 (November 30, 1963): 701–2.

Catholic News Agency. "Bishop emeritus of Gallup Donald E. Pelotte dies at 64." January 8, 2010. http://www.catholicnewsagency.com/news /bishop_emeritus_of_gallup_donald_e._pelotte_dies_at_64/.

Cogley, John. "Catholic Tradition and American Present." *New York Times*, October 30, 1960. http://select.nytimes.com/gst/abstract.html?res =F00610FC3B541A7A93C2AA178BD95F448685F9.

———. "John Courtney Murray." *America* 117 (September 2, 1967): 220–21.

Coleman, John. "The Achievement of Religious Freedom." *U.S. Catholic Historian*, 24, no. 1 (Winter 2006): 21–32.

"Colleges: Kudos." *Time* (June 24, 1966). http://content.time.com/time /subscriber/article/0,33009,835814,00.html.

"Concordat between Pope Pius IX and the Republic of Ecuador (1862)." Concordat Watch. http://www.concordatwatch.eu/showtopic.php?org_id =40037&kb_header_id=47262.

Connell, Francis J. "Catholics and 'Interfaith' Groups." *American Ecclesiastical Review* 105 (November 1941): 337–53.

———. "Christ the King of Civil Rulers." *American Ecclesiastical Review* 119 (October 1948): 244–53.

———. "Discussion of Governmental Repression of Heresy." In *Proceedings of the Third Annual Convention of the Catholic Theological Society of America*, 98–100. Bronx: Catholic Theological Society of America, 1948.

————. "Freedom of Worship." *American Ecclesiastical Review* 149, no. 3 (September 1963): 201–2.

————. "Pope Leo XIII's Message to America." *The Ecclesiastical Review* 109 (October 1943): 249–56.

————. "Reply to Father Murray." *American Ecclesiastic Review* 126 (January 1952): 49–59.

————. "The Theory of the 'Lay State.'" *American Ecclesiastical Review* 125 (July 1951): 7–18.

Costelloe, M. Joseph. "Father Murray's 'Reflections.'" *Homiletic and Pastoral Review* 61 (May 1961): 812.

Curran, Charles. *American Catholic Social Ethics: Twentieth-Century Approaches.* Notre Dame, IN: University of Notre Dame Press, 1982.

Faggioli, Massimo. *John XXIII: The Medicine of Mercy.* Collegeville, MN: Liturgical Press, 2014.

Fenton, Joseph Clifford. "Cardinal Ottaviani and the Council." *American Ecclesiastical Review* 148 (January 1963): 44–53.

————. "Doctrine and Tactic in Catholic Pronouncements on Church and State." *American Ecclesiastical Review* 145 (October 1961): 266–76.

————. "Extra Ecclesiam Nulla Salus." *American Ecclesiastical Review* 110 (April 1944): 300–6.

————. "New Concepts in Theology." *American Ecclesiastical Review* 119 (July 1948): 56–62.

————. "Principles Underlying Traditional Church-State Doctrine." *American Ecclesiastical Review* 126 (June 1952): 452–62.

————. "Revolutions in Catholic Attitudes." *American Ecclesiastical Review* 145 (August 1961): 120–29.

————. "The Catholic and the Church." *American Ecclesiastical Review* 113 (November 1945): 376–84.

————. "The Church and the State of Siege." *American Ecclesiastical Review* 112 (January 1945): 54–63.

————. "The Doctrinal Authority of Papal Encyclicals." *American Ecclesiastical Review* 121 (September 1949): 136–50.

————. "The Holy Father's Statement on Relations between the Church and State." *American Ecclesiastical Review* (November 1955): 323–31

————. "The Proof of the Church's Divine Origin." *American Ecclesiastical Review* 113 (September 1945): 203–19.

————. "The Relation of the Christian State to the Catholic Church." *American Ecclesiastical Review* 123 (September 1950): 214–18.

————. "The Status of the Controversy." *American Ecclesiastical Review* 124 (June 1951): 327–52.

————. "The Teachings of the *Ci Riesce.*" *American Ecclesiastical Review* 130 (February 1953): 117.

————. "Toleration and the Church-State Controversy." *American Ecclesiastical Review* 130 (May 1954): 342–43.

Fesquet, Henri. *Le Journal du Concile.* Foulcalier: Robert Morel, 1966.

Fowler, Glenn. "Philip Scharper, A Publisher, Dies." *New York Times,* May 8, 1985. http://www.nytimes.com/1985/05/08/nyregion/philip-scharper-a-publisher-dies.html.

Gonnet, Dominique. *La Liberté Religieuse à Vatican II: La contribution de John Courtney Murray, SJ.* Paris: Editions du Cerf, 1994.

Granfield, Patrick. "An Interview with Father Connell." *American Ecclesiastical Review* 157 (August 1967): 74–82.

Hooper, J. Leon. "Murray and Day: A Common Enemy, A Common Cause?" *U.S. Catholic Historian* 24, no. 1 (Winter 2006): 45–61.

Hunt, Robert P. and Kenneth L. Grasso, eds. *John Courtney Murray and the American Civil Conversation.* Grand Rapids, MI: Eerdmans, 1992.

Kendall, Willmoore. "Natural Law and 'Natural Right.'" *Modern Age* 6 (Winter 1961–1962): 94, 96.

Kennedy, John F. "Transcript: JFK's Speech on His Religion," at http://www.npr.org/templates/story/story.php?storyId=16920600.

Komonchak, Joseph A. "Murray, John Courtney." In *The Encyclopedia of American Catholic History,* edited by Michael Glazier and Thomas J. Shelley, 993–96. Collegeville, MN: Liturgical Press, 1997.

————. "Ottaviani, Alfredo, Cardinal." In *The Modern Catholic Encyclopedia,* edited by Michael Glazier and Monika Hellwig, 600–1. Revised and expanded. Collegeville, MN: Liturgical Press, 1994, 2004.

————. "Religious Freedom and the Confessional State: The Twentieth Century Discussion." *Revue d'Histoire Ecclésiastique* 95 (2000): 634–50.

————. "The American Contribution to *Dignitatis Humanae*: The Role of John Courtney Murray, SJ." *U.S. Catholic Historian* 24, no. 1 (Winter 2006): 1–20.

————. "'The Crisis in Church-State. Relationships in the U.S.A.': A Recently Discovered Text by John Courtney Murray," *The Review of Politics* 61, no. 4 (Autumn 1999): 675–714.

————. "The Silencing of John Courtney Murray." In *Cristianesimo nella Storia: Saggi in Onore di Giuseppe Alberigo,* edited by A. Melloni, et al., 657–702. Bologna: Il Mulino, 1996.

Love, Thomas T. *John Courtney Murray: Contemporary Church-State Theory.* Garden City, NY: Doubleday, 1965.

Macht, Joshua. "Running Out of *Time*: The Slow, Sad Demise of a Great American Magazine." *The Atlantic* (April 5, 2013). http://www.theatlantic

.com/business/archive/2013/04/running-out-of-time-the-slow-sad
-demise-of-a-great-american-magazine/274713/.

McElroy, Robert W. "He Held These Truths." *America* 192 (February 7, 2005). http://www.americamagazine.org/content/article.cfm?article_id=3995.

McGreevy, John T. *Catholicism and American Freedom: A History*. New York: W. W. Norton, 2003.

McKeon, Richard. "Rhetoric in the Middle Ages." *Speculum* 17, no. 1 (January 1942): 1–32.

McLoughlin, Emmett. *American Culture and Catholic Schools*. New York: Lyle Stuart, 1960.

Meehan, Seth. "From Patriotism to Pluralism: How Catholics Initiated the Repeal of Birth Control Restrictions in Massachusetts." *The Catholic Historical Review* 96, no. 3 (July 2010): 470–98.

Mejía, Alberto Royo. "Recordando al Cardenal Alfredo Ottaviani a los 30 años de su fallecimiento." At Temas de Historia de la Iglesia. http://infocatolica .com/blog/historiaiglesia.php/recordando-al-cardenal-alfredo-ottaviani-1.

Novak, Michael. *The Open Church*. New York: Macmillian, 1964.

Nuesse, C. Joseph. *The Catholic University of America: A Centennial History*. Washington, DC: The Catholic University of America Press, 1990.

O'Brien, Thomas W. *John Courtney Murray in a Cold War Context*. Landham, MD: University Press of America, 2004.

Ottaviani, Alfredo. *Institutiones juris publici ecclesiastici*. Romae: Typis Polyglottis Vaticanis, 1935–1936.

Ottaviani, Alfredo, Antonio Bacci, et al. *The Ottaviani Intervention: Short Critical Study of the New Order of Mass*. Rockford, IL: TAN Books, 1992.

Parsons, Wilfrid. "Intercredal Co-operation in the Papal Documents." *Theological Studies* 4 (June 1943): 159–82.

Pavan, Pietro. "Declaration on Religious Freedom." In *Commentary on the Documents of Vatican II*, Volume 4, edited by Herbert Vorgrimler, translated by Hilda Graef, W. J. O'Hara, and Ronald Walls, 49–86. New York: Herder and Herder, 1969.

Pelotte, Donald E. *John Courtney Murray: Theologian in Conflict*. New York: Paulist Press, 1975.

Portier, William L. "Theology of Manners as Theology of Containment: John Courtney Murray and *Dignitatis Humanae* Forty Years After." *U.S. Catholic Historian* 24, no. 1 (Winter 2006): 83–105.

Quinn, John F. "The Enduring Influence of *We Hold These Truths*." *The Catholic Social Science Review* 16 (2011): 73–84.

Regan, Richard J. *Conflict and Consensus: Religious Freedom and the Second Vatican Council*. New York: Macmillan, 1967.

"Religion: A Man of the City." *Time* (August 25, 1967). http://content.time
.com/time/subscriber/article/0,33009,841042,00.html.

"Religion: Silencing the Outspoken." *Time* (February 22, 1963). http://content
.time.com/time/subscriber/article/0,33009,828041,00.html.

Rouquette, Robert. "La Concile, Le Second Mois de la Troisième Session."
Études (December 1964): 715–32.

———. "Les Derniers Jours de la Troisième Session." *Études* (January 1965):
100–120.

Rynne, Xavier. *The Second Session: The Debates and Decrees of Vatican Council
II, September 29 to December 4, 1963.* New York: Farrar, Straus & Co., 1964.

Scharper, Stephen Bede. "Philip J. Scharper and the Editorial Vocation: Publishing Ideas of Consequence." *American Catholic Historian* 21, no. 3 (Summer 2003): 19–35.

Schuck, Michael J. "John Courtney Murray's American Stories." In *Finding
God in All Things: Celebrating Bernard Lonergan, John Courtney Murray,
and Karl Rahner*, edited by Mark Bosco and David Stagaman, 83–91. New
York: Fordham University Press, 2007.

Shea, George W. "Catholic Doctrine and 'The Religion of the State.'" *American Ecclesiastical Review* 123 (September 1950): 161–74.

Sheed, F. J. "The Sword of the Spirit." *The Ecclesiastical Review* 107, no. 2
(August 1942): 81–92.

Sheridan, Michael P. "Of Many Things." *America* 117 (September 2, 1967): 208.

Sorenson, Theodore. *Kennedy.* New York: Harper & Row, 1965.

Southern, David W. *John LaFarge and the Limits of Catholic Interracialism,
1911–1963.* Baton Rouge: Louisiana State University Press, 1996.

Walsh, Michael, ed. *Dictionary of Christian Biography.* Collegeville, MN:
Liturgical Press, 2001.

Walsh, Michael J. "Ecumenism in War-time Britain: The Sword of the Spirit
and Religion and Life, 1940–1945 (I)." *The Heythrop Journal* 23, no. 3 (July
1982): 243–58.

———. "Ecumenism in War-time Britain: The Sword of the Spirit and Religion and Life, 1940–1945 (II)." *The Heythrop Journal* 23, no. 4 (October
1982): 377–94.

Ward, Barbara. "'Sword of the Spirit' Crusade Is a Clear Call Out of Chaos."
America 67 (August 29, 1942): 566–67.

Weigel, Gustave. "Religious Toleration in a World Society." *America* 90 (January
9, 1954): 376.

Weil, Harry J. "Catching up with Mr. Time." *ARTNews* (April 9, 2013).
http://www.artnews.com/2013/04/09/catching-up-with-time-mag-top
-portraitist/.

Documents of the Magisterium

Benedict XVI. *Message for the Celebration of the World Day of Peace 2011*. http://www.vatican.va/holy_father/benedict_xvi/messages/peace/documents/hf_ben-xvi_mes_20101208_xliv-world-day-peace_en.html.

Francis. Encyclical letter *Evangelii Gaudium* (2013). http://w2.vatican.va/content/francesco/en/apost_exhortations/documents/papa-francesco_esortazione-ap_20131124_evangelii-gaudium.html.

Gregory VI. Encyclical letter *Mirari Vos* (1832). Papal Encyclicals Online. http://www.papalencyclicals.net/Greg16/g16mirar.htm.

John XXIII. Encyclical letter *Pacem in Terris* (1963). http://www.vatican.va/holy_father/john_xxiii/encyclicals/documents/hf_j-xxiii_enc_11041963_pacem_en.html.

John Paul II. Encyclical letter *Redemptor Hominis* (1979). http://www.vatican.va/holy_father/john_paul_ii/encyclicals/documents/hf_jp-ii_enc_04031979_redemptor-hominis_en.html.

Leo XIII. Encyclical letter *Longinqua* (1895). http://www.vatican.va/holy_father/leo_xiii/encyclicals/documents/hf_l-xiii_enc_06011895_longinqua_en.html.

Pius IX. *Syllabus of Errors*. Papal Encyclicals Online. http://www.papalencyclicals.net/Pius09/p9syll.htm.

Pius X. Encyclical letter *Pascendi Dominici Gregis* (1907). http://www.vatican.va/holy_father/pius_x/encyclicals/documents/hf_p-x_enc_19070908_pascendi-dominici-gregis_en.html.

———. Encyclical letter *Vehementer Nos* (1906). http://www.vatican.va/holy_father/pius_x/encyclicals/documents/hf_p-x_enc_11021906_vehementer-nos_en.html.

Pius XII. "The Discourse 'Ci Riesce.'" *American Ecclesiastical Review* 130 (February 1954): 129–38.

Second Vatican Council, *Dignitatis Humanae* (The Declaration on Religious Liberty). *Vatican Council II: The Conciliar and Postconciliar Documents*. Edited by Austin Flannery. Collegeville, MN: Liturgical Press, 2014.

Index